Penelope Winslow, Plymouth Colony First Lady:
Re-Imagining a Life

Portrait of Penelope Pelham Winslow, unknown artist, ca.1651.
Courtesy Pilgrim Hall Museum

Penelope Winslow, Plymouth Colony First Lady: Re-Imagining a Life

by Michelle Marchetti Coughlin

PILGRIM SOCIETY
75 Court Street, Plymouth, Massachusetts

Published by the Pilgrim Society
75 Court Street, Plymouth MA 02360

ISBN-13: 978-0-940628-06-9

Design by: Marie Pelletier

Printed by: Powder Horn Press

To find out more about the Pilgrim Society, visit www.pilgrimhall.org

Pilgrim Society books may be purchased for business or personal use.
For information on sales or bulk purchases, please contact the Pilgrim Society
at shop@pilgrimhall.org.

Cover: Portrait of Penelope Pelham Winslow, unknown artist, England, ca. 1651. Oil on canvas. Gift of Abby Frothingham Gay Winslow, 1883, PHM 0055. *Courtesy Pilgrim Hall Museum.*

This, too, for Mark

Indeed, few challenges to historians in the twenty-first century loom larger than this one: how to integrate, as fully as possible, words and things—verbal and material "documents."

—John Demos, review of *The Times of Their Lives: Life, Love, and Death in Plymouth Colony* by James Deetz and Priscilla Scott Deetz

Contents

List of Illustrations

Acknowledgments

Many talented individuals have kindly given of their time and expertise in the effort to re-imagine Penelope Winslow's life. Particular thanks go to Kimberly Alexander, University of New Hampshire; Peggy Baker; Alan Beales of Bures-online.co.uk; Penelope Pelham Behrens; Edward L. Bell, Massachusetts Historical Commission; Peggy Bendroth, Congregational Library and Archives; the Boston Athenaeum library staff; Francis J. Bremer, director of New England Beginnings; Nancy Carlisle, Historic New England; Executive Director Donna Curtin, Judy Fosdick, and the board and staff of Pilgrim Hall Museum; Nonie Gadsden, Museum of Fine Arts, Boston; Rebecca Griffith, formerly of Pilgrim Hall Museum; Heather and Mike Hargrove, Smallbridge Hall; Nick Humphrey, Victoria and Albert Museum; Brock Jobe, Winterthur Museum; Marshfield historian Cynthia Hagar Krusell; Jade Luiz, Plimoth Plantation; the Massachusetts Historical Society library staff; Kate Ness, formerly of Plimoth Plantation; the New England Historic Genealogical Society; Susan North, Victoria and Albert Museum; Kathleen O'Connor, 1699 Winslow House; Stephen O'Neill, Suffolk University; the Petre family, Ferriers; the Probert family, Great Bevills; Rebecca Shawcross, Northampton Museum and Art Gallery; Beth Wees, Metropolitan Museum of Art; Lauren Whitley, Museum of Fine Arts, Boston.

Special thanks to Rebecca Fraser for generously sharing insights and information about the Winslow and Pelham families and for reading a draft of this manuscript. Many thanks, too, to historians Edith Gelles and Abby Chandler for their kind and insightful feedback. Any remaining errors are the fault of the author's.

Much-appreciated support for a research trip to the U.K. was provided by the Ronin Institute for Independent Scholarship.

Finally, with much gratitude to the extended Marchetti and Coughlin families for their ongoing support and encouragement. It means the world.

Editorial Note

During Penelope Pelham Winslow's lifetime, spelling, capitalization, and punctuation were not standardized and could vary widely. In quotations appearing in this book, they have been preserved as written in order to provide some contemporary "flavor." Dates, however, have been modernized. Until 1752, Great Britain and the Anglo-American colonies used the Roman Julian calendar, which observed the start of the new year on March 25, "Lady Day." Dates between January 1 and March 24 were often recorded in a dual-date system; for example, January 1, 1620/1. In order to prevent confusion, years before 1752 have been adjusted to reflect the transition to the Gregorian calendar, which recognized January 1 as the start of the new year.

Introduction

New England's first permanent settlement, Plymouth Colony was founded in 1620 by English immigrants seeking religious refuge and a better way of life. Plymouth, therefore, holds a crucial place in the origin story of American history. Less well known is that the colony was established at the site of the former Wampanoag village of Patuxet. The place the settlers chose to set down roots was land that the Wampanoag, or "People of the First Light," had called home for many generations.

Although the "Pilgrims" have retained a strong hold on the public imagination, they and others who came to call the Old Colony home remain, in many ways, unknown. Even more anonymous have been the Indigenous peoples who lived in the area for millennia prior to European colonization. Because most early Native and European Plymouth residents alike left behind few personal accounts, their experiences have been difficult to recover. This has been particularly the case with Plymouth Colony's women. Despite the profound impact they had on the region, the lives of both Indigenous and English women have, until quite recently, been largely unexplored.

Long before the English settlers arrived, Wampanoag women had primary jurisdiction over the land. They controlled property and planting grounds and were the main agricultural workers. Inheritance of land passed down through the matrilineal line, and daughters inherited regardless of their marital state. Within their societies, Wampanoag women could hold positions of spiritual authority and tribal leadership, serving as sachems and diplomats.[1]

English women, in contrast, were subject to the all-encompassing system of patriarchy. Laws and customs were based on the perception that women were physically, intellectually, and morally weaker beings and that men should be the primary holders of social, economic, legal, and political power. These attitudes had deep roots in Christian theology, particularly the biblical story of Eve, said to have corrupted Adam and caused humanity's banishment from the Garden of Eden.

Upon marriage, an English woman became known as a *feme covert,* literally a "covered woman," whose individual rights and very personhood were subsumed by those of her husband. Marital property was recognized as being under a husband's control, and any children were to be subject to his authority.

Within this structure, however, women held certain rights and privileges, many of which were expanded in Plymouth as a result of the colonists' religious beliefs. Because a general knowledge of scripture was deemed essential, many girls were taught to read (although the ability to write, a skill associated with the professions, was less common). Under English common law, widowed women were generally allowed "dower rights," typically a third of the couple's personal property and a life interest in a third of the real estate; in Plymouth, this benefit became a right. Plymouth courts allowed women generally equal protection under the law. And ministers promoted marriage as a loving partnership (with wives as "helpmeets" and men holding ultimate authority).[2]

The first English women to voyage to Plymouth were the nineteen who arrived aboard the *Mayflower*.[3] (They were accompanied by eleven girls and teenagers.) Ranging in age from their twenties to around sixty, they hailed from diverse social and economic backgrounds. Eighteen were married, and most were mothers; three were in their final trimester of pregnancy aboard ship. Some had experienced the difficulties and uncertainties of migration before, having pulled up roots in England to settle in Holland.

Only five of these adult women survived the first year in Plymouth: Eleanor Billington, Mary Brewster, Elizabeth Hopkins, Susanna White Winslow, and a young servant named Dorothy. (Elizabeth Hopkins and Susanna White Winslow had given birth while at sea, as had Mary Norris Allerton, who died the first winter following the death of her stillborn child.) All of these women were faced with enormous challenges and responsibilities, having to find ways to make a new life in an alien land for themselves and their families, and also care for the children who had lost parents. They went on to literally help build the colony from the ground up: establishing homes and, in some cases, businesses; raising families; and creating a community.[4]

* * * * *

The lack of attention paid to Plymouth women's lives is partly due to the fact that, until fairly recently, women's activities in general were not considered worthy of study because they typically occurred outside the public domain. The lack of written records they left behind has also proved a deterrent. There are no Plymouth Colony women's diaries that we know of, and few letters. Because Plymouth women, like other women of the time, were not allowed to practice a profession and were denied full legal rights and citizenship, there are a limited number of official documents in which they appear as primary actors.

A general absence from the historical record applies even to the colony's most prominent female residents, including First Lady Penelope Pelham Winslow (1633–1703). A member of the English gentry who was married to Governor Josiah Winslow, she was one of the most influential women in the colony's history—a role model, adviser, and taste maker. She also led a life marked by drama: crisscrossing the Atlantic, narrowly escaping death in a childhood house fire, participating in two pivotal events linked to the outbreak of King Philip's War, and becoming a refugee in the war's wake. Following the early death of her husband, she assumed the responsibility of managing vast landholdings and waged legal battles to reclaim family inheritances. The strength of her legacy had repercussions lasting generations, and may have influenced some descendants to remain loyal to the British Crown during the American Revolution.

Although Penelope Pelham Winslow authored or is mentioned in just a handful of surviving documents, other sources survive to tell her story. Foremost among these is a trove of physical evidence, what is generally referred to as material culture: the array of objects made and used by people. These remnants of Penelope's existence—ranging from surviving homes to treasured personal possessions to shards of pottery—have great value and power in speaking to her experiences. Providing insight into her lifestyle, attitudes, and sense of identity, they also offer a glimpse into the lives of other women of the time and a portal into the world of Plymouth Colony.

An exploration of Penelope Pelham Winslow's life sheds much-needed light on the later years of Plymouth Colony's significant but brief history (it was absorbed by Massachusetts Bay in 1692). It also shifts the focus to women, who remain significantly underrepresented in the telling of America's story. Combining the evidence found in both written and material historical sources—archaeological artifacts; architecture and landscapes; household furnishings; fine and decorative art; personal writings; and court, church, government, town, and probate records—provides the keys to re-imagining her world in all its rich complexity.

Timeline of Penelope Pelham Winslow's Life (1633–1703)

1620:   Plymouth Colony is founded.

1630:   Massachusetts Bay Colony is established.

1633:   Penelope Pelham is born in Bures Hamlet, Essex, England.

1638:   Penelope and her family emigrate to Massachusetts Bay; her mother Jemima dies on the voyage.

1646:   Penelope's family returns to England; she and her brother Nathaniel remain in Massachusetts.

1642–1651: English Civil Wars; "Interregnum" government lasts 1649–1660, with Puritan Oliver Cromwell serving as Lord Protector 1653–1658.

ca. 1651: Penelope marries Josiah Winslow; their portraits are painted in England, along with that of Josiah's father Edward.

1660:   Restoration of the British monarchy

1662:   Sachems Wamsutta and Weetamoo stay at Penelope and Josiah's home.

1664:   Penelope gives birth to her first child to survive to adulthood, a daughter Elizabeth.

1671:   Penelope gives birth to her son Isaac, her second child to survive to adulthood.

1673:   Josiah becomes governor of Plymouth Colony.

1674:   In December, John Sassamon, a Christian minister and member of the Massachusett tribe, appears at Penelope and Josiah's home to warn Josiah of Metacom's plans to attack Plymouth Colony; the following month he is found dead, presumed murdered.

1675–1676: King Philip's War

1680:   Josiah dies in December.

1683:   Penelope submits her deposition in her case concerning family inheritances.

1684:   Penelope's daughter Elizabeth marries Stephen Burton.

1686–1689: Plymouth and other northern American colonies operate as part of the Dominion of New England.

1692: Plymouth Colony is absorbed by Massachusetts Bay.

1700: Penelope's son Isaac marries Sarah Wensley.

1703: Penelope submits her property rights petition to the Massachusetts government.

1703: Penelope Pelham Winslow dies in December in Marshfield.

Pelham/Winslow Family Tree (Abbreviated)

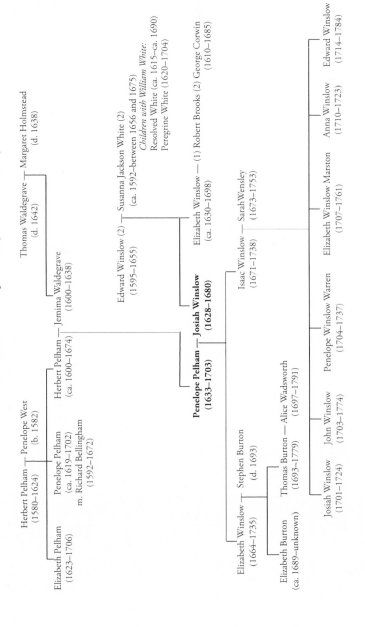

Chapter 1
PRIZED POSSESSIONS

Penelope Pelham Winslow was not a "typical" Plymouth Colony woman. Born in England in 1633, she was a member of the British gentry with an aristocratic heritage extending back generations. On her father's side, she had a royal lineage, descending from Plantagenet kings, Eleanor of Aquitaine, and William the Conqueror. Her paternal third great-grandmother was Mary Boleyn, one-time mistress of King Henry VIII and sister to the doomed queen Anne. Penelope's mother's family, the Waldegraves, had played a part in British government for centuries.[5] Other illustrious relatives included the Baron de la Warr, for whom the colony of Delaware was named; early governors of Virginia; and leading settlers of Massachusetts.[6]

Penelope's father, Herbert Pelham (ca. 1600–1674) was one of Massachusetts Bay's "merchant adventurer" investors, transplanting his family to the fledgling colony in 1638. Within a short time, he acquired large tracts of land and became a civic leader, serving on the colony's Court of Assistants and as Harvard College's first treasurer. Sadly, Penelope's mother, Jemima, died on the voyage to New England.

When, in 1646, Herbert Pelham returned to England along with most of his family, thirteen-year-old Penelope remained behind to launch her own American success story. Her aunt, Penelope Pelham (ca. 1619–1702), and uncle, Richard Bellingham (1592–1672), long-serving governor of Massachusetts (1641, 1654, and 1665–1672), took Penelope's future in hand, overseeing her education and expanding her connections with New England's leading families. Penelope would eventually marry into one of these families: her husband, Josiah Winslow, was the son of Pilgrim leader Edward Winslow and would himself become the first native-born governor of Plymouth Colony.[7]

These brief biographical details provide just the barest outline of Penelope Pelham Winslow's early years. They only hint at the type of person she was and the nature of her experiences. Unfortunately, we can't supplement these facts with insights provided by Penelope's own words from this time, because none have survived. We can, however, begin to better know her through several personal possessions that have withstood the ages. The most compelling of these is undoubtedly her portrait, one of very few that exist of a seventeenth-century American woman (*fig. 1*). Painted in oil on canvas at the time of her marriage to Josiah Winslow, it is a powerful introduction to her story.

The young woman depicted in the painting is striking, with dark eyes and strong features. She is fashionably attired in an off-the-shoulder, olive-green gown with a scooped neck that reveals just a hint of cleavage; her elegantly long fingers clasp a salmon-colored stole about her shoulders. Though both gown and stole are unadorned, their luster makes it clear they are of a rich fabric. Wearing a strand of gold beads around her neck, Penelope has stylishly arranged her fair ringlets and adorned them with a pearl-trimmed hood.[8]

It is tempting to imagine what Penelope might have been thinking when she sat for the portrait, a process that likely took more than one session. This trip to London, perhaps her first, would have given her much to contemplate: the excitement of the city, the opportunity to reconnect with family, the prospect of a new life with Josiah. Penelope's expression is difficult to read. (Could that be the trace of a smile on her lips?) Yet with her head held high and a steady gaze directed at the viewer, she projects an unmistakable air of self-assurance.

Portraits of Josiah Winslow (*fig. 2*) and his father, Edward (*fig. 3*), then in London on Plymouth Colony business, appear to have been painted at the same time. The date "1651" is inscribed on Edward's portrait, timing that also supports Josiah's presence in London. That year the Reverend John Eliot of Roxbury wrote to Edward noting that he happened to see Josiah before his "coming over" to visit Edward. Eliot complimented Josiah on being a "prop^r man of respectfull caryage" who provided "respectfull serviceablenesse unto his moth^r," but also advised him against being "too often at the wine" when taking leave of his friends.[9]

The paintings of Edward and Josiah portray two dark-haired men dressed in expensive black suits and starched white collars secured with gold tassels. Edward's outfit is further distinguished by gold buttons and decorative cuffs. While Josiah—like Penelope, wearing his locks in a long, fashionable style—clasps his right hand over his heart, perhaps in a pledge to his new bride, Edward holds a letter. Signed, "From yr loving wife Susanna," it is an homage to his spouse and fellow *Mayflower* passenger, Susanna Jackson White Winslow.

The painter responsible for the portraits is unknown, but may have been the prolific English artist Robert Walker (1599–1658). Walker's subjects included many who, like the Winslows and Pelhams, opposed the Crown and supported the Puritan Oliver Cromwell-led Parliamentarian forces during England's Civil Wars (1642–1651). Although the Winslows were

"Pilgrims" and the Pelhams "Puritans," their religious views were quite similar. Both were Reformed Protestants committed to the idea that individuals should have a direct relationship with God as mediated through scripture. They also believed in predestination (that only some would experience salvation); in the importance of undergoing a personal conversion experience; in the need to live an upright life; and that even the most ordinary occurrences were part of a divine plan. While Puritans wanted to "purify" the Church of England from its ceremonial excesses and corruptions, the Pilgrims, or "Separatists," wanted to separate from it—a radical approach that attracted far fewer adherents. Both groups regarded New England as a place where they could establish godly communities and a potential New Jerusalem.

Given this background, it is surprising that Penelope's dress, jewelry, and hairstyle clearly reflect the royal influence of Queen Henrietta Maria (1609–1669), French Catholic consort to the lately executed (1649) King Charles I. For many years, Queen Henrietta Maria had held a strong influence on contemporary fashion, discarding the ruffs and stiff styles of earlier decades for more relaxed dress silhouettes, softer colors, and lustrous materials. Favoring more natural hairstyles and jewelry, she popularized ringlets and choker necklaces like those worn by Penelope. The fabric of Penelope's gown and shawl worn in her portrait are strikingly similar to those of the queen depicted as St. Catherine in a pre-1641 painting attributed to Anthony van Dyck (*fig. 4*). Moreover, Penelope's hairstyle, hood, and choker resemble those featured in a mid-seventeenth-century portrait of the queen's daughter, Princess Mary (1631–1660) (*fig. 5*), painted by Gerard van Honthorst (1592–1656).[10] Clearly, Penelope's religious and political convictions did not preclude her from following trends in fashion.

Penelope undoubtedly believed her high-style clothing was fitting for her position as the daughter and wife of gentlemen, and later as Plymouth Colony's First Lady. And to be sure, clothing was integral to the social structure of colonial New England, not to mention the early modern world. Styles of dress maintained social hierarchies, displayed religious and political affiliations, and were a clear indication of an individual's economic status. At the time, what one wore was so important in both England and New England that "sumptuary" laws prohibited people from dressing above their station.[11]

In England, these laws were an attempt to maintain social hierarchies and prevent excessive spending on clothing. In New England, they also took on a "spiritual" dimension, underpinned by the Puritan belief that misrepresenting oneself by dressing above one's class was not only a cultural transgression but an offense to God. Upper-class men and women were permitted more luxurious attire, but they, too, were expected to exhibit modesty and moderation in keeping with the Puritans' general approach to the enjoyment of life's pleasures. Creature comforts such as fine clothing, good food and drink, and leisure time were highly valued and appreciated as gifts from God, but were expected to be enjoyed within limits. Abusing these blessings was perceived as sinful, and as a challenge to the well-ordered, devout society the Puritans strove so hard to create.

Penelope's choice of clothing for her portrait may have been a bit rebellious. The hood she is wearing leaves her hair mostly uncovered; her shawl is draped loosely, leaving her shoulders bare. Instead, she might have opted for expensive clothing that communicated her status, but that was also more plain and modest. Had she been in Boston while the portrait was painted, with friends and family about, she likely would have opted for more demure attire, along the lines of that displayed in wealthy New England women's portraits painted in later decades of the seventeenth century. As Martha Finch has shown, Penelope's appearance reflects a transition in ideas about feminine modesty and "godly plainness" underway in New England by the mid-seventeenth century. As society became more socially and religiously diverse, individuals became less concerned about demonstrating their spiritual commitment through their outward dress.[12]

The three Winslow portraits were shipped back to Plymouth Colony and displayed prominently in the family homes. Visitors would have interpreted them as symbols of their subjects' wealth, status, and significance to the colony. The portraits continue to serve as important representations of early Plymouth, and since 1882, when they were donated by a descendant, have been exhibited at Plymouth's Pilgrim Hall Museum, the nation's leading repository of Pilgrim belongings. Established in 1824, it is considered the oldest continuously operating public museum in the country.

Pilgrim Hall Museum holds a number of Winslow family possessions, including several items that belonged to Penelope. Her portrait, for example, has long been displayed alongside a shoe she is supposed to have worn at her wedding. Made of pigskin covered in salmon-pink silk and embellished with silver "galloon," or silk-covered thread, the wedding slipper, as it has commonly been known, was made in England or France in the mid-seventeenth century.[13] Backless in the style of a mule, it has a chunky 1¼-inch heel and an odd-looking forked toe (*fig. 6*).

The shoe and its mate were said to have been worn by many subsequent family brides but were ultimately separated in the early nineteenth century. As recently as the 1990s, a stir was caused when the descendant-owner of the second shoe discovered its mate's existence at Pilgrim Hall Museum and arranged for both to be exhibited together.[14]

The temporary reunification of the "wedding slippers" reflects an underlying theme in the story of Penelope Pelham Winslow: the continual cropping up of new pieces of information. As in general with our understanding of women's lives in the colonial period, hers is an ever-evolving story as new evidence come to light. Recently, interpretation of the shoes has shifted dramatically with the revelation that they were actually made for a man. Historic footwear experts have confirmed that they were likely the fancy indoor slippers of a gentleman, made around 1660–1680.[15]

In the seventeenth century, highly decorative mules were worn by both sexes, and salmon-pink was a universally popular color. Men's mules of the era can be differentiated by their low, broad heels made of leather and by squared or forked toes, while women's commonly displayed higher, contoured heels and rounded or pointed toes. The Winslow shoes very likely belonged to Penelope's husband Josiah. Ironically, the mule-style shoe at Pilgrim Hall Museum is displayed near Josiah's baby shoes (*fig. 7*).[16]

The story of Josiah owning the shoes may have become lost soon after his death in 1680—not surprising, given that his and Penelope's son Isaac, through whose family the pair of shoes descended, was only nine at the time. Yet its evolution holds several lessons for us. In addition to highlighting the caution that must be used when considering stories passed down with family heirlooms, it also illustrates the importance of shielding historical materials from contemporary ideas about gender-based behavior, roles, and customs.[17]

Although the shoes were not Penelope's, it is possible that she preserved pieces from her wardrobe that remained in the family for generations. Clothing in the seventeenth century was expensive and highly valued, and was often passed down to family members. One early-twentieth-century local historian noted that, in her childhood, she remembered seeing "rich brocade dresses, satin slippers, quilted petticoats, English made corsets and other fine things worn by [Penelope] and sacredly preserved by her descendants." To the writer's mind, this finery appeared "incongruous with the traditional simplicity and poverty of New England life." Such elaborate attire certainly was uncommon in Plymouth Colony. Yet historian Peggy

Baker, who has evaluated the few Plymouth Colony women's wills and inventories that provide details about clothing, has found that, although wardrobes were often limited, they did offer their owners, across the economic spectrum, a range of choices. For example, the probate inventory taken following the 1631 death of widow Mary Ring of Plymouth tells us that she owned white, violet, and "mingled coloured" waistcoats (the top part of a woman's dress); red and violet petticoats; seven aprons (in white, blue, black, and mulberry); three linen caps and two hats; a white and a blue pair of stockings; two pairs of shoes; and a few high-style items, such as stomachers (decorative pieces to fill in a bodice) and ruffs. Her clothing was worth the sizable sum of over £9.[18]

By contrast, the clothing included in the 1687 inventory of the estate of Mary Ring's daughter, Elizabeth Cook of Eastham, was valued at only £3 19s, but included four capes; five petticoats and five shifts; a waistcoat and three "under wastcoats"; a corset; five aprons; seven neckcloths; coifs and head bands; and a silk hood and cap. The low overall value of Cook's wardrobe was likely due to the fact that many of the pieces were "old."[19]

Penelope did not leave a will, and no inventory of her possessions was taken following her death, but some insight into her wardrobe might be gleaned from the inventory of Ann Atwood, the widow of London "gentleman" John Atwood, who died in Plymouth in 1654. Valued at a substantial £27, Ann Atwood's clothing included four gowns, including two of silk; twelve stomachers; eight petticoats (three red and one green); six waistcoats; corsets, shifts, stockings, and hose; numerous neck cloths and head cloths; fifteen caps; a black cloak; two beaver hats; a riding suit; two muffs, one of velvet; five pairs of cotton gloves; a scarf with lace; and twenty-three handkerchiefs, including four lace ones. As Peggy Baker points out, Ann Atwood would have been considered well dressed in any European city.[20]

Penelope's clothing choices may have represented a particularly meaningful way for her to express her self-identity. After her marriage to Josiah, they took up residence in rural Marshfield, located twelve miles up the coast from Plymouth and thirty miles south of Boston (Edward Winslow, who acquired around 1,000 acres locally, had founded the town in 1632). Being descended from British gentry and connected with the ruling elite of Cambridge and Boston, Penelope likely found comfort and reassurance in fine apparel as a reminder of who she was and where she came from.

Penelope's personal style would also have served as a significant act of self-expression, allowing her to display a sense of creativity, demonstrate her familiarity with fashion trends, and highlight her connections to cosmopolitan London. She was well aware that, like all members of society, she would be judged on her appearance. Given her position as one of the most influential women in Plymouth Colony, she would have dressed the part.

Although Penelope likely purchased most of her clothing, she may well have had some skill as a needlewoman if we can believe a story passed down with a purse that is supposed to have been hers. Now housed at Pilgrim Hall Museum, the small reticule-style bag—only four inches square—is ornamented in a geometric design of blue, white, and yellow beads that are possibly Venetian (*fig. 8*). Similar purses—many carrying inscriptions relating to faith, love, and luck—were popular in England in the first half of the seventeenth century. Often they were given as gifts, to men as well as women. If Penelope did indeed make this bag, she may have intended it for Josiah.[21]

The legend that descended with the purse is that Penelope beaded it while on a sea voyage. There is no way to prove this, but if true, it certainly would have helped her pass the approximately two months' passage between England and America. It also would have provided her with a potentially satisfying creative outlet. If Penelope was the bag's creator, she was evidently proud enough of her work to preserve it throughout her lifetime.

While purses like this one are rare in New England, other remnants of Plymouth Colony women's needlework survive. Perhaps the most well known is the sampler made about 1653 by Duxbury's Loara Standish, the teenage daughter of Captain Myles and Barbara Standish (*fig. 9*). A skillful and colorful creation, the sampler is a long and narrow piece of linen ornamented with roses, carnations, and other decorative elements. It carries a standard religious verse: "Loara Standish is my name/Lord guide my heart that I may do thy will/Also fill my hands with such convenient skill/As may conduce to virtue void of shame/and I will give the glory to thy name." Such samplers were common educational tools for girls, providing opportunities to practice the alphabet and learn different stitches, but they also offered a more aesthetic alternative to everyday sewing and mending. Like Penelope's purse, they represent personal expressions of artistry and imagination.[22]

Among the objects at Pilgrim Hall Museum, perhaps that with the most intimate connection to Penelope is a silver, blunt-ended needle known as a bodkin (*fig. 10*). Engraved with the initials "PW" and possessing large eye-holes at each end, it would have been used to draw laces through eyelet holes to tighten a bodice, ribbon through loops to fasten clothing, or tape through a hem. Bodkins were typically made of steel, but sometimes of silver; the 1683 inventory of the estate of a Marshfield neighbor of Penelope's, Margaret Howland, shows that she, too, was the owner of a silver bodkin (along with "two silver thimbles & one parsell of silver buttons"). Although bodkins are primarily associated with women, they were also used by men. This particular piece was made in either England or America in the seventeenth century, so could have been acquired by Penelope in either Boston or London following her marriage.[23]

Applied to practical, everyday purposes, the bodkin reveals a more prosaic side of Penelope's life and connects her to other women of the period (although most women's bodkins were not made of silver). We can imagine her daily routine, begun by donning the many articles of clothing that women then wore: shifts or "underlinen"; petticoats; whole gowns or a two-part combination of waistcoat and skirt; sleeves (which were detachable); and neckerchiefs—not to mention caps, gloves, hoods, cloaks, shoes, stockings, and aprons. While women washed their own underlinen and that of family members, they rarely laundered their skirts or gowns. These standards of cleanliness, or lack thereof, extended to the person as well; it was considered important to keep one's visible body parts—faces and hands—clean, but bathing was not done regularly.[24]

The bodkin would come in handy as Penelope adjusted lacings on her clothing to accommodate pregnancies. In truth, she did not have an easy time bearing children and may have experienced several stillbirths or miscarriages. The vital records tell us that she had a daughter on March 13, 1658, who was buried two days later. They are silent on any additional children until the birth on April 8, 1664, of a daughter Elizabeth (likely named for Josiah's sister), who survived to adulthood. A son, Edward, was born three years later, in May 1667, but died young. In 1671, Penelope gave birth to her second child who lived to adulthood, a son named Isaac. Approximately twenty years had passed since her marriage.[25]

Although the loss of children was not uncommon in Plymouth Colony—or any place in the world at this time—Penelope and Josiah's small family size was unusual. Plymouth was a place of large broods: the first generation saw parents having an average of 7.8 children (with 7.2 living to adulthood); the second generation, 8.6 (with 7.5 living to adulthood); and the third generation, 9.3 (with 7.9 living to adulthood). Plymouth's family structure has been famously described by historian John Demos as a "little commonwealth" modeled on the larger social and political system, with children answerable to their parents, servants to their masters and mistresses, a wife to her husband, and a husband to the local, colonial, and imperial government. All were ultimately accountable to God. Because in the British tradition, political power and landholdings traditionally passed down through families, genealogy held tremendous significance. As historian Karin Wulf has written, lineage was the "platform for hierarchies of status and for access to power."[26]

* * * * *

It is possible Penelope stored her bodkin in an elaborate dressing case that has survived (*fig. 11*). Constructed of pine and covered with an "oyster-shell" walnut veneer featuring an inlaid circular pattern of a lighter wood, the case is a high-style piece not frequently seen in New England. It was likely made in England in the late seventeenth or very early eighteenth century. Measuring approximately 18⅝ inches wide by 14⅝ inches deep by 4⅝ inches high, its hinged lid opens to reveal a framed mirror on the inside cover. A blue-silk-covered interior is divided into a large central compartment and several smaller ones; two still hold handblown glass bottles with silver lids. If the dressing case was indeed Penelope's, she would have found it convenient for storing toiletries, jewelry, needlework tools, writing implements, letters, personal papers, and perhaps even books. Complete with a lock, it would have offered a secure and private space to keep valuables and personal mementos and would have served as a useful traveling case.[27]

Penelope is said to have passed down the dressing case, along with the information that she brought it back with her from London in 1651, to her son Isaac's daughter Penelope. But these events cannot be true, since Penelope senior died in 1703, a year before her granddaughter was born, and the case dates from decades later than 1651. The younger Penelope does appear to have owned the case, however, passing it down to her own daughter, Sarah Warren Sever, in whose family it descended.[28]

These surviving objects represent just a fragment of those Penelope owned and used during her lifetime. But they begin to fill in some of the unknown corners of her life, and allow her an opportunity to "speak" for herself. They provide some solid foundations on which to begin to build her story.

Chapter 2

AT HOME IN THE OLD AND "NEW" WORLDS

Penelope's personal possessions give us some sense of her as an individual and a physical being. Material culture related to the houses in which she lived offers a fuller picture of her personal environment and connects her to varied aspects of contemporary family, social, economic, and political life. Starting with her childhood home in England, these spaces provided a comfortable setting for her daily activities, communicated her high status to society, linked her with community and local government, and held layers of personal meaning.

Penelope's earliest home, a surviving three-story, sixteenth-century manor house called Ferriers, in Bures Hamlet, Essex, England, was brought to her parents' marriage by her mother Jemima Waldegrave. Ferriers was not as grand as the nearby mansion owned by Jemima's parents, Smallbridge Hall (*fig. 13*), which, complete with moat and deer park, was spacious enough to entertain Queen Elizabeth I and her large entourage in 1561. (A mulberry tree still living on the property is said to have been planted at the queen's behest to mark her visit.) Yet Ferriers was without question an impressive dwelling. Set in a spreading landscape that served as a constant visual reminder of how much property the family owned, it was a spacious family seat (*fig. 12a*). Comprising three floors, it included a "Great Parlour," "Little Parlour," hall, kitchen, pantry, and dairy; bedrooms—or "chambers"—above these rooms; and garret, or attic, rooms above those. Also on the property was a "meale" house to store grain, a brewhouse, and a sixteenth-century courthouse (*fig. 12b*) likely used by the Waldegraves to resolve local grievances. As a local justice of the peace, Herbert Pelham may have used it, too. Although Penelope lived in the house for just a few years before emigrating to New England, the property remained very important to her.[29]

The hamlet of Bures lay in the picturesque Stour River Valley (in later centuries painted by such well-known artists as John Constable and Thomas Gainsborough), in a region known as East Anglia. Located roughly seventy miles from London and ten from the ancient market town of Colchester, Bures was twenty miles from the North Sea. Penelope's maternal family's roots ran deep in this area, and ancestral homes dotted the landscape for miles. The local church, St. Mary's, featured Waldegrave-funded expansions and prominently displayed family tombs; it was where Penelope herself was baptized on April 25, 1633.[30]

When in 1638, as a five-year-old, Penelope arrived in the Massachusetts Bay Colony with her father and four siblings—Waldegrave, Jemima, Nathaniel, and Katherine—they took up residence in what is now Cambridge.[31] A political, religious, economic, and intellectual center located across the Charles River from Boston, the town was home to the new Harvard College. By 1639 it would have the colony's first printing press. The Pelhams' home had formerly belonged to Simon Bradstreet and his wife Anne Dudley Bradstreet (1612–1672), America's first published poet.[32] The family attended the Congregational Church led by Rev. Thomas Shepard, who hailed from Earles Colne in Essex, close to Bures.

The Pelhams set up housekeeping with more furnishings than the average settler, thanks to Penelope's mother's parents, Thomas and Margaret Waldegrave. The Waldegraves, along with two of Penelope's cousins, had originally intended to emigrate with the Pelhams and had arranged for the sending of "divers goods[,] chattels[, &] moneys" to New England. They had been forced to turn back when Margaret fell sick and later died, but many of the "provisions of great value" made it over. Although an exact list of these items has not survived, their original total value was estimated by Thomas Waldegrave as having been at least £1,400.[33]

A year after the Pelhams' arrival, the widowed thirty-nine-year-old Herbert married the twenty-one-year-old widow Elizabeth Bossevile Harlakenden; Herbert had known Elizabeth's first husband, and perhaps Elizabeth herself, back in England. The Pelhams moved into the Cambridge home of Elizabeth and her two young daughters near the town landing.[34] They lived there only briefly, however, as in December of 1640 the home was almost destroyed by fire. Former governor John Winthrop recorded the dramatic incident in his journal:

> Mr. Pelham's house in Cambridge took fire in the dead of the night by the chimney. A neighbor's wife hearing some noise among her hens, persuaded her husband to arise, which, being very cold, he was loth to do, yet through her great importunity he did, and so espied the fire, and came running in his shirt, and had much to do to awake any body, but he got them up at last, and so saved all. The fire being ready to lay hold upon the stairs, they had all been burnt in their chambers, if God had not by his special providence sent help at that very instant.[35]

The family was not homeless for long; Herbert Pelham was one of the largest property owners in Cambridge. By 1642 he owned four houses and over 900 acres in the colony, including a 600-acre farm. Yet it may have taken seven-year-old Penelope some time to recover from the trauma of their having narrowly escaped being "burnt in their chambers." Making an impression on her, too, would have been the sense that they had been spared by a "special providence" from God (and a fortunately persistent neighbor woman). Given the Puritan worldview in which all events were perceived as being part of a divine plan, this deliverance would have inspired in the family a feeling of deep gratitude, but also, perhaps, a sense of specialness. The consequences of the fire could so easily have turned catastrophic; the fact that everyone in Herbert and Elizabeth's large blended family was saved was truly miraculous.[36]

Harvard College, founded in Cambridge in 1636 primarily to train the clergy, formed an important backdrop to Penelope's youth (*fig.14*). Although she herself could not attend—Harvard would not award degrees to women until more than three centuries had passed, in 1963—threads connecting her to the college run throughout her story. Her father, of course, held the prestigious position of the school's first treasurer, serving 1643–1650 (part of which time he was overseas). As one of the founding members, along with Edward Winslow, of the Society for the Propagation of the Gospel in New England, created to spread Christianity among the Natives, Herbert Pelham was also linked with the founding of Harvard's Indian College. (The Indian College's first building, erected circa 1655, was only the second building on Harvard's campus.) Twenty-first-century archaeological excavations conducted near the former Indian College have uncovered pieces of printing type, reflecting Native involvement with the college's press. The press was responsible for the first Bible printed in British North America, in 1663, Rev. John Eliot's translation into the North American Indian language family of Algonquian.[37]

After most of Penelope's family returned to England, her brother Nathaniel, just a year older, remained behind to attend Harvard, graduating in 1651. He was likely the channel through which Penelope first became acquainted with Josiah Winslow, who attended Harvard but did not graduate.[38] Josiah's father and her own were known to each other, but became closer in the late 1640s while both were living in England.[39] Many years later, Penelope's younger half-brother Edward would make the voyage from England to America so he, too, could attend Harvard, graduating in 1673. A rather wild young man, Edward got into some trouble at the college and owed the school money. When Herbert Pelham made his will in 1673, he stated that Edward was only to receive certain rental income if he could acquire certification from the Massachusetts or Plymouth governor and four assistants that there had been a "real change in him for the better" and that he had grown "Serious, Sober & Solid."[40]

Harvard's influence on Penelope was more than just that she was connected with men who attended the school or held positions there. In fact, it is possible she absorbed some of her brother Nathaniel's education. Although very few writings in her hand survive, a deposition and a government petition concerning the retrieval of family lands, which she authored later in life, demonstrate a facility with language and a familiarity with the law. Several documents carry her signature, indicating a high level of literacy. (Although most New England girls were taught to read, fewer learned how to write, a skill associated with the "masculine" pursuit of business.) Moreover, in his will her father left her half his library.[41] Penelope certainly understood the value of an education—even as she realized the avenues for pursuing learning were quite different for girls than boys.

* * * * *

In 1646, Herbert Pelham was asked by the Massachusetts General Court to tend to colony business back in England. He requested that he be excused from this responsibilty but ended up returning anyway, because he needed to tend to an estate issue. He had inherited property from his former father-in-law, Thomas Waldegrave, who had since passed away, but a dispute had arisen over the distribution with Isaac Wincoll, husband of Thomas's daughter Mary. The fate of Ferriers and other valuable property was in question. Although Herbert originally intended to return to New England, he never did. Within a few years of his arriving back in England, the British monarchy had been overthrown and the Puritan government led by Oliver Cromwell held the reins of power. The Interregnum (period between reigns) of 1649–1660 offered opportunities for advancement, as Herbert's current father-in-law, Colonel Godfrey Bossevile, served in the new Parliament. Herbert himself would become a member of Parliament in 1654.[42]

Prior to departing, Herbert or Penelope's stepmother Elizabeth would have given her parting advice on how to conduct herself; Penelope's behavior would of course reflect on the family. This counsel may have taken a form similar to that dispensed in 1680 by Elizabeth Ward Saltonstall to her twelve-year-old daughter Betty, then on a visit to a family friend:

> Carry your self very respect[fully] and dutyfully to…Mrs Graves as though she were your mother and likewise respect[fully] and lovingly to the children and servants….[B]e sure you keep your selfe diligently imployed either at home or at

schoole as Mrs Graves shall order…. [M]ake it your dayly worke to pray earnestly to God that he would keepe you from all manner of evill. [T]ake heed of your discourse att all times that it be not vaine and foolish…. [B]e sure [to] follow your reading[;] omit it not one day, your father doth purpose to send you some Coppies that so you may follow your wrighting likewise.[43]

Before her family sailed, Penelope likely moved into the upscale Boston residence of her aunt Penelope and uncle Richard Bellingham. Although the couple were among the colony's leading elite, their marriage in 1641 had raised eyebrows. According to John Winthrop, Penelope senior "was ready to be contracted to a friend of [Bellingham's], who lodged in his house,… when on the sudden the governor treated with her, and obtained her for himself." The couple, who were both from Boston, England, had likely previously known each other, but were separated in age by more than a generation. Bellingham excused his actions on the basis of the "strength of his affection, and [the fact] that [Penelope] was not absolutely promised to the other gentleman." Yet he caused further scandal by not publicizing the marriage banns and performing the ceremony himself. Although New England Puritans had eliminated the ritualized, religious aspect of weddings, making them civil affairs officiated by magistrates rather than ministers, Bellingham certainly acted illegally by performing his own ceremony. He also broke the law in failing to post the "banns," or announcement of the upcoming marriage. Because of his position as governor, however, he ultimately escaped serious censure.[44]

Penelope Pelham Bellingham was about twenty-seven when the thirteen-year-old Penelope joined her household. The records tell us that, from an early age, the senior Penelope was committed to the Puritan experiment. As a sixteen-year-old, she had made the voyage to New England independently, and as a young adult, she had become a full member of the First Church of Boston. At the time of her death in 1702, Boston judge Samuel Sewall, who served as a pallbearer at her funeral, observed that she had been "a vertuous Gentlewoman, *antiquis Moribus, prisca fide*" (roughly translated, "of ancient customs, of ancient faith").[45] Penelope Bellingham's faith would have stood her in good stead as she gave birth to, and subsequently lost, several children in the 1640s and 1650s—an example of stoicism the younger Penelope perhaps drew upon as she later shared this experience. Penelope Bellingham would have overseen the remainder of Penelope's education, as well as teaching her the skills needed to run a household. As a colonial First Lady herself, she would have served as a role model of appropriate behavior: dignified, genteel, charitable, and supportive of her husband.

Penelope's uncle Richard *(fig. 15)* was in his mid-fifties and an imposing figure. In the years he was not serving as governor, he held other prominent positions, such as deputy governor or assistant on the governor's council. Known for being religiously orthodox, he opposed the practices of Baptists and Quakers, despairing of their insubordination and believing "their Religion is to speake rebellion and sedition in the presence and to the face of authority." Politically, he advocated for a code of laws and rights, and was one of a committee who drafted the colony's first legal code, the Body of Liberties, in 1641. (The Body of Liberties ensured a number of civil "rights, liberties, and privileges…to be respectively, impartially, and inviolably enjoyed," but also formally legalized slavery.) An opinionated and outspoken individual, he was immortalized in such nineteenth-century fiction as Nathaniel Hawthorne's *Scarlet Letter* and Henry Wadsworth Longfellow's *New England Tragedies.*[46]

The Bellinghams' stone "mansion house" was an impressive and well-known residence in the center of town, and would have exposed Penelope to people and ideas that exponentially broadened her world.[47] Boston was a town on the rise during her years of residence. Although the Great Puritan Migration (approximately 1620–1640) had come to an end with the outbreak of the English Civil Wars, Boston's population and influence were expanding. By the mid-1600s it had become the geographical capital of Atlantic Puritanism. It was also developing as a robust center of trade due to what historian Mark Peterson has described as "the commercial and political initiative of its leadership class."[48]

One companion Penelope would have had at the Bellingham house was her aunt Elizabeth Pelham (1623–1706), sister to her father and Penelope Pelham Bellingham, who never married. Just ten years older than young Penelope, Elizabeth remained connected to her throughout her life. It is quite possible Elizabeth served as Penelope's chaperone when she returned to England around the time of her marriage to Josiah. Elizabeth had, like her sister Penelope, braved the Atlantic crossing from England alone. She showed the same courage navigating the world as a single woman, earning the respect of those around her.

Chapter 3

"THE FESTIVE & SOCIAL BOARD AT CARESWELL"

We don't know exactly where or when Penelope married Josiah Winslow; the circumstances of their courtship and wedding remain a mystery. Since indications are that their portraits were painted in London in 1651, it is quite possible they were married in London, too, perhaps living there for a time afterwards. This "honeymoon" period had to come to an end, however, as Josiah had responsibilities back home in Marshfield. As the couple braced themselves to undertake the ocean crossing, Penelope also would have prepared herself for her new life in Plymouth Colony, perhaps anticipating the challenges and opportunities her new circumstances presented.

After having lived in the elegant Bellingham home and spending time in fashionable London, Penelope must have endured an adjustment period when she and Josiah settled in quiet Marshfield. They first resided in Josiah's childhood home, which Edward Winslow had named "Careswell" after his family's English estate. Living there, too, was Josiah's mother Susanna, who by this time had become an icon of Plymouth Colony history. One of only five adult *Mayflower* women to survive the first winter, Susanna had earlier escaped religious persecution in England to live in Amsterdam. There she married her first husband, William White. She and William had made the *Mayflower* voyage with their young son Resolved. While aboard ship in Provincetown Harbor, Susanna gave birth to the first Pilgrim child born in New England, a son named Peregrine, Latin for "pilgrim." (A cradle Susanna is believed to have brought from Holland for Peregrine is displayed at Pilgrim Hall Museum; *fig.16*.) After William White died during the first winter, Susanna married Edward Winslow in the colony's first wedding.

Susanna herself had served as a Plymouth Colony First Lady when Edward Winslow was governor in 1633, 1636, and 1644. (She would ultimately be distinguished by having been both wife and mother to governors.) After Edward returned to England for the final time on diplomatic business in 1646—ironically, on the same ship as the Pelhams—Susanna was left to oversee their large Marshfield estate. In 1655 Edward died at sea while on a military mission to Hispaniola in the Spanish West Indies. Afterwards, Susanna successfully petitioned the British government for the balance of his salary to satisfy debts he had accrued in London and provide her with a "subsistence."[49] A true survivor, Susanna had learned many life lessons that Penelope would have found helpful to heed.

As Penelope and Josiah started married life, Josiah launched his military and civic career. During the decade of the 1650s, he was elected captain of the Marshfield militia; a member of Plymouth's governing body, the General Court; a United Colonies commissioner; and Myles Standish's successor as the colony's military leader. Penelope's social connections in Marshfield and Plymouth Colony broadened, and her status increased as Josiah took on more and more of a leadership role, becoming governor in 1673. Even as a newcomer, however, Penelope's position as a person of importance was assured. In addition to having married into one of the colony's leading families, she brought her own pedigree as a member of the gentry, the daughter of Harvard's first treasurer, and the niece of the Massachusetts governor. During Penelope's lifetime, the social hierarchy was so important that class could outweigh gender in determining an individual's social and political power; despite the tradition of patriarchy, high-ranking women could potentially wield more influence than men of lower status.[50] Wherever she went, Penelope would have been treated with deference and respect.

During her first years in Plymouth Colony, these positive developments in Penelope's life were somewhat overshadowed by instances of personal tragedy. In August 1657, her older sister Jemima, married since 1654 to the Reverend Samuel Kem of Albury, England, died at the age of twenty-seven. The very week of Jemima's death, the Reverend Ralph Josselin had recorded in his diary that, "their never was a more sickly time generally in England then now." In September, Josselin noted that the community held a public fast "in regard of the general visitacon [visitation] by sicknes, which was a feavour and ague [an illness marked by fever, chills, joint pain] very mortal in some places." Three months prior to her death, Jemima had been experiencing some type of religious crisis while visiting her family back in Bures. Josselin, who had "preacht" in Bures on May 7, noted in his diary that he had spent time "with Mrs Keam who is under feares, and endeavoured to persuade her to rowle her soule on god in christ." Jemima may have been estranged from her husband, as she died in Bures.[51]

In 1657 Penelope also lost her brother Nathaniel, whose vessel disappeared while on a voyage back to England. This loss was widely felt; as the Reverend Daniel Gookin described it, "Mr. Garrett's ship…had aboard her a very rich lading of goods, but most especially of passengers, about fifty in number; whereof divers of them were persons of great wor[th] and virtue, both men and women; especially Mr. [Thomas] Mayhew [minister to the Indians on Martha's Vineyard], Mr. Davis, Mr. Ince, and Mr. Pelham, all scholars." Nathaniel, who had been accompanied by his Harvard classmate John Davis and Jonathan Ince of the prior year's class, was only twenty-five.[52]

Just a few months following the loss of her brother and sister, on March 13, 1658, Penelope gave birth to a daughter, whose name went unrecorded. The baby died two days later. Finally, that fall Penelope's stepmother Elizabeth died back in Bures, a victim of the "sickliness of the time."[53]

The 1650s also saw the passing of some of New England's most influential leaders. Back in Boston, the charismatic John Cotton senior, teacher of the First Church, where Penelope had attended services with the Bellinghams, passed away in 1652. Nathaniel Morton, the long-serving Secretary of Plymouth Colony, expressed the feelings of many when he wrote that "An influence of good, not only flowed from him unto the church over which he was set, but also into all the churches in New England." And in 1657, legendary Pilgrim leader and veteran governor William Bradford died. Josiah, who had not long ago lost his own father, was moved to compose a poem to commemorate the loss of this esteemed patriarch: "And how God made [Bradford] an instrument/To us of quiet peace and settlement/I need not speak; the eldest, youngest know/God honor'd him with greater work than so…. And for our better progress in this course/Let now our great necessity enforce/Each man to study peace, and to improve/His greatest strength to reunite, in love/The hearts and affections of us all/Lest by our faults, God's work to th' ground should fall."[54] With the passing of the first generation of New England leaders, power was increasingly being taken over by members of the second generation like Josiah.

Penelope's father himself was celebrated in a poem in the 1650s, in Edward Johnson's *Wonder-Working Providence of Sion's Savior in New England.* Published in London in 1653, Johnson's work was an early history of New England from a Puritan perspective. One chapter opened by celebrating the arrival in Cambridge of the "much honoured Mr. Herbert Pelham, a man of a courteous disposition, humble, and heavenly minded," and included a poem acknowledging Herbert's efforts to help New England's cause overseas, but also lamenting his failure to return to Massachusetts: "Harbertus, hye on valiant, why lingerst thou so long?/Christs work hath need of hasty speed, his enemies are strong:/In wildernesse Christ doth thee blesse with vertues, wife and seed/To govern thou at length didst bow to serve Christs peoples need/To thine own soyle thou back dost toyle, then cease not lab'ring there/But still advance Christs Ordinance, and shrink no where for feare."[55] One wonders how Penelope may have reacted to this public tribute to her father—and whether she, too, had mixed feelings about his failure to return. Since the passing of her brother Nathaniel, she alone represented his "seed" left in the "wildernesse" of New England.

Penelope and Josiah's generation faced a host of both internal and external challenges. The decades of the 1650s and 1660s brought droughts, crop failures, smallpox, threats of war with the Dutch, fears of possible Indian insurrection, provocations by the Quakers. Many ministers proclaimed that these difficulties were punishments from God for New Englanders' "backsliding," or loss of spiritual commitment and growing preoccupation with worldly ways. Anxious that New England would not fulfill its mission of becoming a New Jerusalem, they preached frequent "jeremiads," or lamentations over the loss of collective mission. Declining church admission in the mid-seventeenth century seemed to confirm their fears. The institution of the 1662 Halfway Covenant, by which the children of baptized church members who had never undergone a conversion experience were themselves allowed to become church members, was perceived by many New Englanders as a confirmation of failure. (Yet, as historian Virginia DeJohn Anderson has pointed out, declining church membership in the mid-1600s may have been a reflection that many in the second generation were still too young to join, and that some Puritans were over-scrupulous about deciding whether they had attained a true state of conversion.)[56] The pressure Penelope and Josiah's generation faced in feeling worthy of the sacrifices made by the New England settlers was profound.

* * * * *

Penelope and Josiah's house, like other dwellings of the period, was a stage on which both "private" and "public" life was acted out, a space in which families engaged in a variety of domestic, economic, and civic activities. Josiah would have conducted his commercial enterprises from the home, as well as military and government business. Occasionally Penelope partici-pated in these affairs, as when in the 1660s she witnessed a contract between William Barstow of Scituate and Josiah and Constant Southworth, acting for Plymouth Colony. A second witness was Sarah Standish, likely Sarah Alden Standish of Duxbury, the daughter of John and Priscilla Mullins Alden and daughter-in-law of Myles and Barbara Standish. This particular agreement concerned the maintenance of a North River bridge that would allow access to northern areas of Plymouth Colony and beyond, an important piece of infrastructure business. Such an example underscores the fact that, although local women were not making laws or running the government, they were participating on a daily basis in activities that strengthened the colony.[57]

When Josiah traveled on personal or colony business, Penelope would have acted as a "deputy husband" in his stead. Laurel Thatcher Ulrich has explored this role, in which the colonial American housewife, who was conversant with her husband's business activities because most took place at home, would have been accepted by other men as a suitable substitute when her husband was not available. In her role as "consort," a wife was expected to support her husband's work; a husband, in turn, trusted his wife to act in his best interest. As Ulrich notes, "under the right conditions any wife not only *could* double as a husband, she had the responsibility to do so." Described in the words of contemporary Thomas Fuller, a woman "in her husband's absence, is wife and deputy-husband, which makes her double the [results]…of her diligence. "At his return[,] he finds all things so well he wonders to see himself at home when he was abroad."[58]

In addition to running her household, raising her family, and overseeing property and business affairs when Josiah was away, Penelope would have spent much of her time administering hospitality. Given the social mores of the time and the distances often involved in travel, visitors—particularly those of the upper classes—would have expected to be offered food and drink and a gracious welcome. The author of the nineteenth-century *Historical Memoir of the Colony of New Plymouth* wrote of the family's hospitality that it was "not only generous, but (according to the notions of the age) magnificent. In addition to [Josiah's] military and civil distinctions[,] he had acquired that of being the most accomplished gentleman, & the most delightful companion, in the colony." The chronicler added that, "the attractions of the festive & social board at Careswell were not a little heightened by the charms of [Josiah's] beautiful wife." Although no first-hand observations regarding Penelope's personal appeal seem to have survived, the characterization of her as a charming hostess was perpetuated through the years; in fact, an undated twentieth-century note in the Pilgrim Hall Museum object file for her portrait states that she "was known for her beauty, culture, and hospitality at the Winslow estate."[59]

In her role as hostess, Penelope was not merely entertaining guests, she was wielding real power. She could control visitors' access to Josiah, mediate the messages given to him, and exert influence over political allies and opponents. By the same token, other women likely sought her out on an informal basis on their husband's behalf. As historians have shown, the rituals involved in hospitality not only maintained social order, but provided women with an opportunity to effect social, political, and economic outcomes.[60]

Penelope's social role also would have had a more relaxed and private aspect, allowing her to spend time with friends and acquaintances. These women would likely have been of the highest social rank; generally, wives of the colony's male leaders and ministers. Sarah Alden Standish, for example, who was close to Penelope's age, may have been paying a social call when she and Penelope were asked to witness the North River bridge contract. Penelope may also have been friendly with Mary Smith Glover Hinckley (1630–1703), wife to Josiah's long-time assistant governor (and eventual successor) Thomas Hinckley. Said to have been a woman of many virtues, Mary was described by the Reverend Samuel Angier as "divine." At the time of her death, her grandson, Rev. Thomas Prince, effused that she had "shone, in the eyes of all, as the loveliest and brightest woman for beauty, knowledge, wisdom, majesty, accomplishments, and graces throughout the Colony."[61]

We do know Penelope had a relationship with Joanna Rossetter Cotton (1642–1702), wife of Plymouth's Reverend John Cotton junior (the son of Penelope's former minister of the same name), because Cotton's letters mention visits. The daughter of a physician, Joanna Cotton was highly educated and became a respected midwife and healer among both men and women, colonials and Native Americans. When living on Martha's Vineyard, she had practiced "Phisicke and Surgery" among the Wampanoags. Throughout her life, Joanna continued to consult medical works she received from friends and relations in England.[62] Her surviving letters reflect a sensitive, spiritual, and intelligent individual.

✶ ✶ ✶ ✶ ✶

After Edward Winslow's 1655 death, Josiah inherited the bulk of his father's property. At some point afterwards—the exact date is unknown—he and Penelope built a home of their own, a suitable place to entertain and conduct colony business. This house no longer stands, but like Penelope's other residences, it was a symbol of family power, social capital, and local civic authority. Since 1940, it has been the site of several archaeological excavations. That year, Henry Hornblower, a recent Harvard graduate who went on to establish the outdoor living-history museum Plimoth Plantation, led a dig on what he believed to be Edward Winslow's former home site. In later decades, archaeologists' close examination of the related artifacts revealed that they dated from the third and fourth quarters of the seventeenth century—reflecting that the home site had been Josiah and Penelope's, not Edward and Susanna's.[63]

In a paper published in 2003, Karin Goldstein, then Curator of Original Collections at Plimoth Plantation, re-examined Hornblower's meticulous drawings in light of subsequent advances in the understanding of seventeenth-century New England timber-framed construction. She found that the structure was originally a rectangular building thirty-six feet long by twenty-seven feet deep, with a rectangular offshoot that was possibly a shed. Indications were that the house was a spacious two-story building with a "hall," where most daily living took place, opposite a more formal parlor on the first floor. Along the rear of the building were a kitchen and dairy. The second floor contained rooms for sleeping; the largest, the hall chamber, would have been used by Penelope and Josiah. (Following Josiah's death, appraisers who inventoried the home's furnishings noted that this room contained the "widdow[']s bed.") The house also appears to have featured a two-story central projection known as a porch, often present on homes of the English minor gentry at the end of the sixteenth century. As Goldstein noted, the style, which was adapted by the New England elite, remained a status symbol throughout the seventeenth century. Those owning houses with porches in Massachusetts Bay included Governor John Winthrop.[64]

The probate inventory taken following Josiah's death in 1680 offers a glimpse inside the house. Unfortunately, it is less detailed than many others of the period, and conspicuously absent are Josiah's land holdings, bequests made in his will, possessions considered Penelope's, and the portraits. Despite these omissions, the appraised worth of Josiah's personal estate was over £360, around ten times that of the average personal estate outside Boston for the whole colonial period.[65]

Books were highly prized by the couple; Josiah's library, perhaps complementing the one Penelope inherited from her father, was worth a hefty £31. Unfortunately, the appraisers did not itemize the titles, so we don't know the full nature or extent of the library. A selection would have been inherited from Edward Winslow, and many would have been of a religious nature. Pilgrim Hall Museum has a copy of James Ussher's 1645 catechism *A Body of Divinite, or, the Summe and Substance of Christian Religion* inscribed by Josiah, and in his will Josiah gifted Marshfield's Reverend Samuel Arnold "such books of divinity as he now hath of mine in his possession

and yᵉ anotations on the bible by the as[s]embly of English divines."
Literacy was highly valued in Plymouth Colony, and library collections,
while rare and expensive, were treasured. Those colonists who did own
books re-read, discussed, and shared them, and counted them among
their most cherished possessions.[66]

Women as well as men took an interest in books. Surviving Plymouth
Colony probate records tell us that men and women gifted books to each
other; that well-to-do widows sometimes expanded upon their late husbands'
libraries; and that women owned books in their own right. These were
often preserved for posterity. *Mayflower* passenger Elizabeth Tilley Howland,
for example, made bequests to family members of religious works and
"great" and "small" Bibles, hoping to share and perpetuate the writings
that had so deeply influenced her life.[67]

The appraisers who made the household inventory following Josiah's death
did not need to assess the value of everything in the house; because of
Josiah's wealth, there was little chance items would need to be sold to settle
debts. But also, the inventory's cursory nature suggests that the appraisers
went through the home quickly, perhaps trying to be respectful of Penelope's
privacy; in fact, the lack of an entry for the hall chamber indicates that
they did not even enter her bedroom other than to note the presence of
her bed. The parlor, for example, is listed as containing "cubbards[,] chairs
[&] *other things* (emphasis added)"; several rooms end with this vague
phrase. The parlor also likely housed the £45 worth of silver plate listed,
along with Penelope and Josiah's portraits. The hall appears to have held a
table, cupboard, trunk, chairs, cases, a carpet, "& other things." A "middle
kitchen" contained an expensive array of pewter and brass. Glasses and
earthenware were stored in the cellar. The parlor chamber included three
beds and furniture (worth £12); also on the second floor were a middle
chamber with "two beds and furniture & other things" worth half the parlor
chamber contents (£6) and a porch chamber with one bed and furniture
and a chest with "co[a]rse old linnin" (£5). A garret with a bed "and other
things" worth only 15 shillings is likely where servants slept.[68]

The silver, brass, and pewter mentioned in the inventory would have been
used in Penelope and Josiah's extensive entertaining. Many of these pieces
would have been of high style, communicating their status to visitors. In
fact, some surviving items show that the Winslows were early to embrace
the move toward domestic and personal refinement that developed in the
seventeenth century and expanded in the eighteenth. The habits of sitting

on benches and eating from communal bowls were replaced with a new fashion for individual matching dishes and chairs. As Karin Goldstein has pointed out, the family may have been the owners of the earliest surviving individual place settings in New England, a group of pewter dishes engraved with the Winslow coat of arms.[69] The chairs mentioned in the inventory, too, may have been part of a matched set. This individualized, genteel approach to home furnishings is further underscored by a surviving "Great Chair" at Pilgrim Hall Museum. Made in Marshfield between 1650 and 1700 of American red oak, it is constructed of joined panels, a more expensive option than a turned chair, and originally would have included a cushion covered in a fine fabric (*fig. 17a*). The chair's formal, decorative carving provides it with a stately air, and to be sure, it would have served as a symbol of authority.[70]

Probate records and surviving possessions help us re-imagine the contents of the Winslow home and also provide information about other residents of the household. Josiah's will for example, mentions both Penelope's aunt Elizabeth Pelham (to whom he gave two mares as a small token of his respect) and Penelope's "companion" Elizabeth Gray (to whom he bequeathed a cow, should she marry or leave Penelope's service). Elizabeth Pelham likely split her time between Marshfield and the Boston home of her sister Penelope. We know she was living in Marshfield in the early 1670s, when she helped Josiah witness deeds. Elizabeth Gray (born ca. 1658) was the daughter of wealthy Plymouth merchant Edward Gray and Josiah's cousin Mary Winslow (the daughter of his uncle John and aunt Mary Chilton Winslow). Josiah and Penelope may have taken Elizabeth in following her mother's death circa 1663–1665.[71] Josiah's reference to her as Penelope's "companion" indicates that she was a specialized attendant. Traditionally, a lady's companion was of a privileged background, a retainer in a household rather than a servant. She would have performed some of the duties of a "lady's maid"—for example, helping Penelope dress and taking care of her clothing—but she also would have acted as a personal assistant. The role of lady's companion developed out of the tradition of noble women having ladies in waiting.[72]

As Susanna Winslow aged, she had her own "companion" to assist with her care, Elizabeth Thomas (born 1652). Elizabeth was the daughter of Careswell's steward, John Thomas (1621–1699), who had arrived in Plymouth as a fourteen-year-old orphan aboard the *Hopewell* and been taken in by Susanna and Edward.[73] In earlier times, Susanna may have lodged other young women under special circumstances. For example, in 1643, John Jenney of

Plymouth noted in his will that he wished his daughter Abigail, in her early twenties and wanting to marry Henry Wood, should first spend a year with Scituate's Rev. Charles Chauncy (who would become president of Harvard), but if Chauncy was "against it, then [he] would have her dwell wth mrs winslowe of Careswell the said terme of one yeare ffurther."[74]

Penelope and Josiah's household also included William White, the young adult son of Josiah's half-brother Resolved. (In his will, Josiah specified that William, likely working on the estate, be given "a feather bed[,] boulster[,] Rug[,] blankett[,] and a paire of sheets at what time he shall leave my wife & family.") Josiah's other half-brother, Peregrine, and his family lived nearby, as did Edward Winslow's brothers, Kenelm and Josiah, and their families.

Edward and Susanna had employed outside help beginning with the two male servants they and their first spouses had each brought over on the *Mayflower*. Additional information on their servants is provided by a 1634 indenture agreement, in which Edward released William Hamonds and Nicolas Prestman from their term of service in exchange for £5. Hamonds and Prestman evidently did agricultural work, as the indenture's terms dictated that they were not to exit their service until the harvest had been brought in.[75]

Josiah and Penelope had servants, too. They would have had to, to farm the land, take care of livestock, handle chores on the property, and help with the household work and child care. Because of the number of visitors the couple received, Penelope would have always needed quantities of food and drink on hand and assistance serving.

Testimony given in the 1655 investigation of the accidental death of a young laborer named Henry Drayton provides a look inside "downstairs" life at the Winslows'. After having stayed out late "fowling" one day in December, Drayton had asked to stay overnight at Careswell. There he "sup[p]ed with the servants" and spent the night in their quarters. The next morning, despite the servants' protests that it was too cold to resume hunting, Drayton left after they had gone "in to [their] dewtyes." (He subsequently died of exposure.)[76] This anecdotal evidence, combined with archaeologists' findings about the home's layout, attests to the fact that some rooms were intended for the family and others assigned to the hired help.

Although on a grander scale, the Winslows' home was like many others in colonial America, with servants, apprentices, visiting relatives, and guests making for a busy setting. Households were not self-sufficient—even from the earliest days, items needed to be purchased, bartered for, or imported—but they were nevertheless social and economic hubs and hives of activity.[77] Today, the Winslow home site gives little hint of the constant traffic it must have seen; it is a quiet place that has been largely reclaimed by nature. But countless clues found beneath the landscape's surface reveal more of its former inhabitants' stories.

Chapter 4
EXCAVATING MEANING

Historians are increasingly making use of archaeological findings in their work, having discovered that these materials help them offer a more integrated, holistic picture of past lives and communities. In what was formerly Plymouth Colony, there is a long tradition of historical archaeological investigation—ranging from nineteenth-century antiquarian efforts to the early professionalism of Henry Hornblower to the twentieth-century mastery of James Deetz. Today, these efforts continue, as seen by the partnership between Plimoth Plantation and the University of Massachusetts Boston's Fiske Center for Archaeological Research, which in recent years has located the original Plymouth settlement site, and work by groups such as the Plymouth Archaeological Rediscovery Project. Plimoth Plantation's newly developed Center for Seventeenth-Century Studies should provide further opportunities to make use of local findings.

The thousands of artifacts that have been uncovered at the Winslow home site over the years provide an invaluable resource for learning about the family, as well as the world in which they lived. Supplementing the details found within written records and the insights gleaned from surviving personal possessions, the archaeological evidence offers another piece of the interpretive puzzle. Together, these sources paint a picture of both everyday routines and larger moments in the lives of Penelope and her household.

Penelope's portrait, purse, and bodkin provide us with clues about her sense of style and needlework abilities. Sewing- and clothing-related artifacts found in the excavations reveal a host of related items and tools she may have used: buttons, hooks and eyes, a "goffering" for ironing ruffles, fragments from sewing and embroidery scissors, and pins. Particularly compelling is a fine bone needlecase with its contents intact. Although these artifacts cannot be positively identified as Penelope's, they date from the period of her residence and there is a strong possibility that at least some were hers. Since women of every status used a needle and thread, whether for everyday sewing or fancy embroidery, these artifacts reflect an aspect of the experiences of all women in the household, whether mistress or servant.

Supplementing the story of Josiah and the silk slipper at Pilgrim Hall Museum—and his shared interest with Penelope in expressing his elite status through high style—are the ornate buckles, brass buttons, and fancy spurs found at the site. Josiah would have used these accessories not only to enhance his appearance, but to give it weight and authority. The inventory taken following Josiah's death tells us that, altogether, his "purse [or cash] & Rings & Apparell & watch" were worth a substantial £54. (One of the rings mentioned was likely the seal ring with the Winslow coat of arms depicted in Edward Winslow's portrait.) In his will, Josiah distributed some of these items to family members: a "su[i]t and cloak" to his half-brother Resolved White, his "spannish rapier [sword] and buffe belt with silver Claspes" to his half-brother Peregrine White, and the pocket watch he inherited from his father to his sister Elizabeth.[78]

Other excavated objects help us glimpse a variety of aspects of seventeenth-century life: two double-sided combs represent the challenges of maintaining personal hygiene; the side with the finer teeth was probably used to pick out lice.[79] A "seal-top" spoon, used as both an eating utensil and a tool for sealing letters with wax, symbolizes the volume of correspondence that originated from the home, particularly after Josiah became governor. A clay marble and a silver "pap" spoon, used to feed infants, evoke the lives of the Winslow children, as does a silver whistle with the initials "EW," which may have belonged to Penelope and Josiah's daughter Elizabeth. A less refined way of making music is embodied in a mouth harp, a folk instrument perhaps misplaced at the site by one of the family's servants.

A host of items provides extensive evidence of the family's dining habits. A large number of milk pan fragments and bottles attest to the presence of a dairy, which provided milk and cheese. Animal bones tell us that they ate lots of beef, some pork and sheep, and surprisingly little fish given their proximity to the sea.[80] Surviving utensils tell us how they consumed this food. A variety of spoons—one with a strong pattern of wear on the left side, showing the user had been right-handed—were found on the site, along with ivory- and bone-handled knives. (The fork was not yet widely used in the colonies.)

Pieces of fine dishware and curtain rings speak to the family's domestic refinement. The latter would have been used for bed hangings, costly fabric of dyed wool or perhaps crewelwork embroidery used to provide privacy and warmth. These panels would have hung on a four-poster wooden bed that may have even featured a "tester," or wooden top. Bed hangings were sometimes referred to as bed "furniture" and were often more highly valued than the bedsteads themselves. The inventory taken following Josiah's death notes that, in addition to the "widdows bed," the family had six beds with furniture.[81]

A wide range of ceramic fragments found on the Winslow home site illustrates the system of cross-cultural exchange that thrived in seventeenth-century America. Shards of European ceramics link the Winslows to the crafts, manufacturing, and trade of the larger Atlantic world. They are complemented by a surviving Delft fruit or finger bowl, ornamented with a swan and tulips in blue, yellow, and green; imported from the Netherlands in the late seventeenth century, it is said to have descended through the family and is currently held by Pilgrim Hall Museum (*fig. 17b*). Remnants of Native pottery reveal a connection with Indigenous peoples. It is entirely possible that Penelope, like her neighbors, cooked on both imported wares and Native-made pots, whichever item suited a particular occasion.[82]

This exchange and adaptation of daily technology went both ways, as evidenced by the finding of a spoon handle filed to a point by a Native person to be made into a new tool (*fig. 18*). Surviving brass and copper fragments from pots acquired in colonial trade reflect that they had been refashioned by Native peoples into projectile points or items of adornment. Native ceramics and European items like straight pins and shot found in recent excavations revealing the Pilgrims' first settlement site on Plymouth's Burial Hill have indicated that the colonists and Wampanoag peoples interacted and were engaged in trade from the early seventeenth century. As these artifacts demonstrate, in many ways, the story of early America was one of accommodation and adaptation.[83]

Despite these Native-settler exchanges, it is evident from an ancient shell midden (covered by a colonial trash pit) on the site that Indigenous peoples had occupied the property long before the Winslows. Among items they left behind were shards of pottery, pestles, and projectile points. A Native presence spanning thousands of years has been widely documented in Marshfield; the area's many natural resources—rivers, marshes, woodlands, fields, and coastline—had much to recommend it. Excavations conducted townwide have revealed a variety of artifacts, including tools, pipes, and ceramics. Such findings are invaluable in telling the story of a people who left behind few written records, and who have so often been misrepresented in the writings of others.[84]

Mayflower passengers John and Priscilla Alden, like Edward and Susanna Winslow, settled on land that had formerly been occupied by Native Americans. As archaeologist Ed Bell somewhat ironically observes, when the Aldens chose the site it was likely already "cleared or lightly forested, and offered the same pleasant setting that had been appreciated by generations of Wampanoag families." Projectile points found on the property may date as late as the seventeenth century, indicating a close overlap of residence. Given the continuation of a Wampanoag presence in the area, Bell speculates on the possibility that Priscilla Alden and other female household members exchanged folk knowledge and technologies with Wampanoag women about medical remedies, culinary traditions, or skills such as sewing and weaving.[85]

Several objects found on the Winslow property highlight Josiah's commercial enterprises and their wider impact. A brand with the initials "HP" used to mark casks and small boxes may well have belonged to Penelope's father Herbert Pelham, for whom Josiah served as New England business agent. A bale seal for cloth—fine fabrics such as "Damask, Diaper, holland and other Linnen" appear in Josiah's inventory—recalls the overseas trade he conducted with the help of his English brother-in-law, Robert Brooks. (A clothing manufacturer and merchant, Brooks and Josiah's sister Elizabeth likely met while she was staying with her father in London in the 1650s.) A surviving "Memorandum" Josiah wrote in late 1656 notes that he sent Brooks beaver pelts, iron, and large barrels of West Indian sugar; Brooks in return was to arrange for Josiah to receive £200 worth of various types of cloth from other merchants, as well as "powder, shot, nails and scythes' and some of [Brooks's] own cloth." Josiah also referred to the fact that he had given Brooks notice that he "had sent £100 worth of goods to the Berbadase [Barbadians] to be consigned to him."[86]

The mention of beaver pelts in Josiah's memorandum speaks to his involvement with the lucrative North American fur trade, an enterprise launched almost as soon as the *Mayflower* landed. As early as 1625, Josiah's father Edward and others from the colony made an expedition to the Maine frontier to explore fur trading possibilities, returning with 700 pounds of beaver pelts. Trading posts were set up in promising locations. In 1628, Edward Winslow, William Bradford, and six other Plymouth leaders took over the colony's £1,800 debt with its investors in exchange for a six-year monopoly on the fur trade. In the early decades, the trade proved profitable for both the settlers and Native peoples; however, eventually some Natives became dependent on European trade goods with the result that a percentage among the younger generation lost the ability to make traditional tools. The insatiable European desire for beaver furs also drove the beaver population to near extinction.[87]

Josiah's memorandum tells us, too, of his participation in the booming sugar trade and business dealings with merchants from Barbados—an island whose economy was based on slavery. The £77 worth of "neat" cattle included in his estate inventory may provide a further connection to the slave trade; although Plymouth sold cattle to Massachusetts Bay, in the later decades of the 1600s it also began selling beef and livestock to West Indian sugar plantations.[88] In general, New England's economy was deeply tied to commercial exchanges with Caribbean plantations. It has been estimated, in fact, that by the 1680s, more than half the ships docked in Boston Harbor on any given day were involved in the West Indian trade.[89]

Unlike many of their social peers in Boston, or even Marshfield, Penelope and Josiah do not appear to have had African slaves, although their descendants would become dependent on the institution of slavery. For their part, Edward and Susanna Winslow at one time were the owners of a male Indian indentured servant named Hope. In 1648, Susanna, serving as Edward's agent, sold ten years of Hope's service to a Barbadian merchant named John Mainford (or "Mainfort").

The deed transferring Hope's indenture was facilitated by Massachusetts Bay Governor John Winthrop. The previous year, Winthrop had received a letter from Barbadian planter Richard Vines informing him that Mainford would be coming to Massachusetts to buy provisions for the island. The sugar trade had become so lucrative that planters avoided taking their slaves' time away from its production to grow crops. As Vines wrote, "Men are so intent upon planting sugar that they had rather buy foode at very deare rates than produce it by labour, so infinite is the profit of sugar…." Colonies like Massachusetts capitalized on this opportunity, providing supplies that included dried cod, a cheap food source for slaves.[90]

The situation for slaves growing the sugar cane was dire: they were expected to work long hours in extreme heat under dangerous conditions, using machetes and spending hours in the "boiling house," where the crop was processed. Slaves were exposed to infectious disease and inadequately fed, clothed, and housed. With its extremely high mortality rates, Barbados was known as a deathtrap.[91]

It has been suggested that the Winslows' servant Hope had been taken captive as a child during the Pequot War (1636–1638), during which many Native women and children were enslaved or forced into indentured servitude.[92] If so, Hope may have been close to Josiah's age, growing up alongside him and spending more than a decade with the family. This begs the question, why would Susanna sell Hope overseas? Having herself endured the pain of separation from friends and family when she left England and later Holland, why would she tear Hope away from everything he had ever known? The answer likely lies in the opportunity for profit. Although the indenture agreement that Susanna arranged with Mainford does not specify the amount she received from the sale, it does note that she had been provided with "good and valuable Consideration." Hope's consignment to service in Barbados poses a sharp contrast to Josiah's position at this time; as Hope was deprived of his liberty, Josiah was poised to become a Plymouth freeman, invested with full civil and political rights.

In the agreement Susanna and John Winthrop fashioned to transfer Hope's indenture, they built in what they perceived as protections. Hope's service was limited to ten years, and he was identified as being subject to "the Orders and Customs of English servants in the said Iland," as opposed to being grouped with other Indian slaves. Yet there would be no way of enforcing these limitations, and Mainford was given the option of transferring Hope's indenture to any "executors [or] Assignes" who were English. Hope had no protection from working in the killing fields of sugar cane or becoming lost in the slave system.[93]

To date, no further records of Hope's existence have been found, and his fate is unknown. His name comes down to us today as a cruel irony—but not, it's worth noting, an unusual one.

Chapter 5
WAR AND REFUGE

The Winslow family—and New England as a whole—had a complex relationship with Native peoples. The celebrated story of Edward Winslow's friendship with the Wampanoag leader we know as Massasoit is a central part of the Pilgrim story. The Plymouth colonists were initially grateful for the support and protection of the Wampanoag people; however, the relationship of the two groups eventually frayed as the result of cultural conflicts. These tensions were exacerbated by the colonists' desire to settle new lands and their belief that God had ordained their presence in New England.

The efforts of Josiah and other high-status, second-generation Plymouth settlers to expand their property holdings certainly added to Native disillusionment. Two deeds witnessed by Penelope's aunt Elizabeth Pelham in Penelope and Josiah's Marshfield home in June of 1672 speak directly to this situation. One concerned the sale of lands that had originally been a portion of the "Major's Purchase," a controversial acquisition made by Josiah (Major Winslow) and other proprietors as "first-born children of [Plymouth's] gov[ernment]." Josiah had been commissioned to act on their behalf and acquired large tracts from sachem "Josias Chickatabutt allies [alias] Wampattucke" in 1662.[94]

The second deed involved the sale of approximately 100 acres by Tuspaquin, a son-in-law of Massasoit who was known as the Black Sachem of Nemasket, and his son "Mantowapact allies [alias] William" to Josiah and his kinsman Edward Gray. The land transfer was meant to satisfy a debt of a little more than £10 owed by Mantowapact to Josiah, which arose over the sale of a horse. Father and son had been forced into a corner after Josiah had sued Mantowapact for £20 for nonpayment of the debt, and Mantowapact, as the court records note, "having nothing to pay but by the sale of some land."[95]

Josiah did not have his father's diplomacy when dealing with Native peoples, nor did he share his close relationships with Native individuals or try to approach them on their own terms. When Edward Winslow first arrived in Plymouth, he had gone to the effort of trying to learn Native languages and had been an interested student of their ways. Josiah, on the other hand, viewed the world as being organized in a hierarchical fashion with Indigenous peoples on a level far below his own. Although he did not appear to bear personal hostility toward them (at least, not prior to King

Philip's War), he believed they should accept their place in this hierarchy and live by the colony's laws and customs. As loyal subjects to the king, they should obey him as the king's local representative.[96]

The charged situation in Plymouth reached a climax in 1675, with the outbreak of King Philip's War. A devastating conflict between New England settlers and members of Eastern Native tribes led by Massasoit's son Metacom, known by the settlers as Philip, the war remains the deadliest per capita in American history.[97] It was the defining event of Josiah's governorship.

It is significant—and has gone largely unremarked—that Penelope was a firsthand witness to two events that helped ignite the war. The first took place in 1662, before Josiah became governor, when as a military leader he was sent to escort Metacom's brother Wamsutta (also known as Alexander), then chief sachem of the Wampanoag, to the Plymouth court. Wamsutta had been accused of having sold land contrary to the terms of a treaty and of conspiring with the Narragansetts against the colonists. Surviving accounts differ as to the nature and sequence of events; however, it appears that in the process of sorting out the charges, Wamsutta and his wife and fellow sachem Weetamoo, along with some of their kin, accompanied Josiah to his and Penelope's home to spend the night.

Penelope was used to her house being used as a satellite seat of government —and likely treated her visitors with hospitality—but hosting such a large group of Native peoples was certainly a unique occurrence.[98] Also compelling to consider is that Weetamoo, by virtue of being a *saunkskwa,* or female sachem, "outranked" Penelope. While Penelope certainly exercised power and influence, Weetamoo was an official leader of her community. One of the "rock women" on whom her tribe depended for diplomacy, Weetamoo served as an ambassador to other Native communities and to colonial authorities. Like Penelope, she, too, had a kinship network that conferred additional authority; Weetamoo's mother, for example (whose name has gone unrecorded), had herself been a saunkskwa, and Weetamoo's sister Wootonakanuske was married to Metacom.[99]

Unfortunately, Wamsutta and Weetamoo's stay at the Winslows' did not go well, as Wamsutta became seriously ill. Josiah summoned local doctor Matthew Fuller to relieve Wamsutta's discomfort, but Fuller's treatments may have actually harmed his patient. Wamsutta's family took him home, where soon afterwards he died. Weetamoo, Metacom, and many others in local Native communities believed Wamsutta had been poisoned, perhaps by Josiah or Matthew Fuller.

Twelve years later, at the end of December 1674, during Josiah's governorship, John Sassamon, a Harvard-educated Native adviser to then-sachem Metacom, appeared at Josiah and Penelope's home to warn Josiah of Metacom's plans to attack Plymouth Colony. It is quite possible Penelope spoke with him and afterwards discussed the serious nature of his visit with Josiah. Sassamon told Josiah he came at great personal risk, that Metacom would kill him should he discover his betrayal. Josiah, however, ultimately did not believe Sassamon's claims. He had recently received similar warnings from other Christian Indians, which had not borne results.[100]

In fear for his life, Sassamon appears to have gone into hiding. In January 1675, his body was found in Assawompsett Pond, near present-day Middleboro, Massachusetts, where he served as minister to local Native Christians. Given his recent warning, it was assumed by the colonists that Sassamon had been murdered. In June, three Native men with connections to Metacom were tried by the Plymouth court, found guilty, and executed. Josiah presided over the trial. Although six of "the most indifferentest, gravest[,] and sage Indians" (including a man named Hope) were called in to consult with the jury and agreed with the verdict, most Natives were outraged, believing the matter should never have gone before a colonial court. (Native people's crimes against other Natives were customarily tried by Indigenous communities; however, because of this particular case's ramifications and occurrence in the colony's jurisdiction, Plymouth opted to take control.)[101]

Just a few weeks following the trial, Penelope was among the first to learn the terrible news of the war's outbreak. On the morning of June 21, a messenger arrived at her home to inform Josiah about Metacom's warriors' attack on the village of Swansea. Homes had been looted and burned, and although no one had been killed, violence was believed to be imminent. Josiah reacted immediately, ordering troops to pursue Metacom and sending news of the assault to Massachusetts Bay Governor John Leverett. Over the next few days, Josiah and Penelope's home became a military command center, as messengers delivered dispatches and Plymouth Colony officials and neighbors came seeking news. Events took a deadly turn following a second attack on Swansea on June 24, in which nine colonists were killed and two others mortally wounded.[102]

A flurry of correspondence over the next few weeks reveals that "tidings" were being issued from and delivered to the Winslows' house at all hours. The first "post from Swanzy" arrived at "break of the day" on June 21; on June 28, when the sun was just "an hour high," Josiah scrawled a hasty report to Captain John Freeman; in a July 18 letter to Captain James Cudworth, he mentioned a post that had come the previous night. On June 27 and July 6 letters arrived for Josiah from Captain Cudworth and Governor Leverett carrying the legend, "haste[,] haste," communicating their urgency. (The latter was written at "2 [o']clock in [the] morning.") As Josiah himself observed, he was in the "constant action of receiving or despatching posts or orders." During this time, his and Penelope's home was in a high pitch of activity and anxiety, particularly as news arrived of raids on other Plymouth Colony towns. Soon these attacks would spread to Massachusetts Bay.[103]

In light of the war's intensification, and Josiah's belief that Metacom personally would seek revenge on him, he wrote his will. He also made arrangements for Penelope and their children to seek refuge. Writing to Governor Leverett on July 26, he noted, "My person, I hear, has been much threatened. I have about twenty men at my house; have sent away my wife and children to Salem, that I may be less encumbered; have flankered my house and resolve to maintain it so long as a man will stand by me." This was not Josiah's first experience dealing with fears of a personal reprisal; in 1671, during an earlier disagreement between Plymouth and Metacom, he had heard rumors that 200 Indian warriors had gathered to kidnap then-governor Thomas Prence and himself and ransom them for a large sum and a favorable peace treaty, but that their plans had been thwarted.[104]

Josiah and the local militia fortified the family's Marshfield home. Lingering traces of these volatile times unearthed at the site by archaeologists lend an immediacy and an impact to the narrative provided by the documentary record. Postholes show that a fence or defensive platform had surrounded the house. The date of numerous pipe stems found on the property coincides with this time period, reflecting that they may have been left behind by soldiers on guard. Quantities of ammunition, pieces of armor, and gun fragments, including a barrel and bone pistol grip, provide evidence of Josiah's ample defenses.[105]

It appears Susanna Winslow had passed away by this time, as Josiah did not mention her in his will or his letter about sending his family to Salem. Penelope and her children—eleven-year-old Elizabeth and four-year-old Isaac —fled to the safety of the home of Josiah's sister Elizabeth and her husband, merchant George Corwin (*fig. 19*), in Salem.[106] (The couple had married following the death of Elizabeth's first husband, Robert Brooks.) Like thousands on both sides of the conflict, they became refugees. Although

Figure 1. Portrait of Penelope Pelham Winslow, unknown artist, England, ca. 1651. Oil on canvas. Gift of Abby Frothingham Gay Winslow, 1883, PHM 0055. *Courtesy Pilgrim Hall Museum.*

Figure 2. Portrait of Josiah Winslow, unknown artist, England, ca. 1651. Oil on canvas. Gift of Abby Frothingham Gay Winslow, 1883, PHM 0054. *Courtesy Pilgrim Hall Museum.*

Figure 3. Portrait of Edward Winslow, unknown artist, England, ca. 1651. Oil on canvas.
Gift of Abby Frothingham Gay Winslow, 1883, PHM 0944. *Courtesy Pilgrim Hall Museum.*

Figure 4. Portrait of Queen Henrietta Maria as St. Catherine, by Matthew Snelling, 1649
(after Sir Anthony van Dyck), *Courtesy Collection of the Duke of Northumberland, Alnwick Castle.*

Figure 5. Portrait of Princess Mary Stuart, Princess of Orange (1632–1660) by Gerrit van Honthorst. *Courtesy National Trust.* The fabric and colors of Penelope's shawl and gown are similar to those worn by Queen Henrietta Maria; her hairstyle and hood bear a strong resemblance to those of Princess Mary.

Figure 6. Winslow Shoe, England or France, ca. 1660–1680. Silk, leather, wood, silver thread. Gift of Richard S. Watson, 1885, PHM 147a. *Courtesy Pilgrim Hall Museum.*

Figure 7. Josiah Winslow Baby Shoes, The Netherlands or New England, 1600–1650. Leather. Loan of the Misses Whitman, 1880s, PHM L145.2. *Courtesy Pilgrim Hall Museum.*

Figure 8. Winslow Beaded Purse, Europe, ca.1600 –1650. Glass beads, silk. Gift of Mary Hayward Havermayer, 1902, PHM 0140. Attributed to Penelope Pelham Winslow. *Courtesy Pilgrim Hall Museum.*

Figure 10. Winslow Bodkin, engraved "P. W," New England or England, ca. 1650–1700. Silver. Ownership attributed to Penelope Winslow. Gift of Misses Whitman, before 1898, PHM 145. *Courtesy Pilgrim Hall Museum.*

Figure 11. Winslow Dressing Case, Boston or England, ca. late seventeenth or early eighteenth century. Burled walnut, yellow pine, oak, silk. Gift of Charles W. Sever, 1893, PHM 143. Believed to have belonged to Penelope Winslow. *Courtesy Pilgrim Hall Museum.*

Figure 9. Loara Standish Sampler, Duxbury, Massachusetts, ca. 1653. Made by Loara Standish (ca.1640–d. before 1655). Linen with silk thread. Gift of Lucius Alden, 1844, PHM 108. *Courtesy Pilgrim Hall Museum.*

Figure 12a. Painting of Ferriers by English artist John Nash, 1962, showing the estate's expansive acreage. *Courtesy Charles Robinson.*

Figure 12b. Courthouse on the Ferriers property. *Courtesy Alan Beales.*

Figure 13. Smallbridge Hall, manor house of Penelope's Waldegrave grandparents. The original building is believed to have been much larger, and was surrounded by a moat and deer park. *Courtesy Alan Beales.*

Figure 14. Engraving of Harvard College, *A prospect of the Colledges [sic] in Cambridge in New England,* attributed to John Harris after William Burgis, 1726. First state, with hand coloring. *Courtesy Massachusetts Historical Society.* This earliest known image of Harvard College depicts Harvard Hall (left), built 1674–1678; Stoughton Hall (center), built 1698; and Massachusetts Hall (right), built 1720, which still stands. Stoughton Hall was built with bricks from the dismantled Indian College.

Figure 15. Portrait of Richard Bellingham by William Read, 1641. Miriam and Ira D. Wallach Division of Art, Prints, and Photographs: Print Collection, New York Public Library. *Courtesy New York Public Library Digital Collections.*

Figure 16. Peregrine White Cradle, The Netherlands, ca. 1620. Wicker, oak, maple. Gift of Catherine Elliott Sever and Charles Sever, PHM 0945. Susanna Jackson White Winslow is said to have brought this cradle on the *Mayflower* for her son, Peregrine White. *Courtesy Pilgrim Hall Museum.*

Figure 17b. Winslow Delft Plate, The Netherlands, 1660–1700. Tin-glazed earthenware. Bequest of Martha Hatch, 1959, PHM 1247. This Dutch plate was passed down through the Winslow family. *Courtesy Pilgrim Hall Museum.*

Figure 17a. Winslow Wainscot Joined Chair, Plymouth or Marshfield, Mass., 1630. Red oak. Gift of Abby Frothingham Gay Winslow, 1881, PHM 0944. This seventeenth-century great chair was a Winslow family possession. *Courtesy Pilgrim Hall Museum.*

Figure 18. Winslow Archaeological Artifacts. The pattern of wear on this spoon indicates that the owner was right-handed. The spoon handle beside it was filed to a point by a Native person to be made into a new tool. These items were unearthed at the Winslow home site. *Courtesy Plimoth Plantation.*

Figure 20. Winslow Mourning Ring, John Coney (1655–1722), Boston, Mass., ca. 1680–1690. Gold, hair. Penelope is said to have commissioned this ring following Josiah's death. *Courtesy Pilgrim Hall Museum.*

Figure 19. Portrait of Captain George Corwin, 1675. Artist probably working in Massachusetts Bay Colony. Oil on canvas, 49 x 39 inches (124.46 x 99.06 cm). Bequest of George Rea Curwen, 1900.4134.1. *Courtesy Peabody Essex Museum. Photo by Jeffrey Dykes.*

Figure 21. 1703 Petition of Penelope Pelham Winslow to the Massachusetts Governor and Council. *Courtesy of the Massachusetts Archives.*

Figure 22. Gravestone of Elizabeth Pelham, Winslow Burial Ground, Marshfield, Mass.

Figure 23. Gravestone of Elizabeth Winslow Burton, Center Cemetery, Pembroke, Mass.

Figure 24. Isaac Winslow House, Marshfield, Mass. The house built by Penelope and Josiah's son Isaac circa 1699, now a historic house museum. (Rear additions were added later.)

Figure 25. Commemorative stone marking the site of the former Winslow homes, Marshfield, Mass. The inscription notes only that Governors Edward and Josiah Winslow lived there, not Susanna White Winslow or Penelope Pelham Winslow.

Penelope must have realized that staying in Salem was the wisest course given the possibility her house would be attacked, abandoning her husband and her home may have been one of the hardest things she ever had to do.

Penelope could expect a warm welcome from the Corwins, as the paper trail indicates the two families were close. Moreover, in 1670 Elizabeth Corwin had named her first daughter Penelope; Penelope in turn had previously named her daughter Elizabeth. As one of the town's—and the colony's—wealthiest families, the Corwins could offer Penelope and her children a comfortable and safe haven.

Although seventeen years later the community of Salem would become ruptured by witchcraft accusations—Jonathan, George Corwin's son by his first wife, would actually serve as a trial judge—during King Philip's War, it was relatively peaceful, some distance away from most of the raids. Nevertheless, residents were concerned enough to build a half-mile-long palisade and strengthen the town's fortifications.[107] During the war, George Corwin, who headed Salem's militia, served as a commanding officer of a troop from Essex County. Although it is not clear how much active service he saw, his involvement certainly brought the conflict closer to home.[108] For Penelope and her sister-in-law Elizabeth, the war must have been an all-encompassing subject of thought and conversation.

In addition to coping with the very real fear of the war's violence, New Englanders also contended with the overwhelming feeling of guilt that they were being punished by God for their sins. As Rev. John Cotton junior wrote, "Gods Anger burns ag[ain]st this poore land[;] what will become of us?" To atone, Plymouth Colony and Massachusetts Bay observed frequent days of fasting and humiliation throughout the conflict; Connecticut observed weekly fast days.[109]

Despite Penelope's family's good fortune in being secure with the Corwins, later indications are that her wartime experiences took a great emotional toll on her. She must have constantly worried about Josiah's safety. As Reverend Josiah Cotton, son of John Cotton junior, later acknowledged, Josiah experienced "many escapes in perilous fights and dangerous voyages."[110] In November 1675, Josiah was appointed commander-in-chief of the United Colonies' forces. For several months that winter, he was on campaign in Rhode Island, during which time he and his soldiers suffered from severe cold and a lack of supplies. As one chronicler described it, "our Horses were tired, our Men faint and our Victuals spent: Insosmuch that several Horses were killed and eaten, whereof the General (the worthy Josiah

Winslow, Esquire, Governor New London [sic]), eat his Part and in all[;] as well hardships and dangers, was not wanting to encourage his Men by his own valiant Example." The narrator also noted in an earlier account that "Many of our Souldiers are troubled with the Flux [dysentery], of which our General is one."[111]

Unfortunately, no letters between Josiah and Penelope have survived. Their correspondence during this period would have been particularly valuable for providing insight into contemporary events and the nature of their relationship. Perhaps an idea of the content of letters they exchanged during the war may be gleaned from the correspondence of Josiah's assistant governor, Thomas Hinckley, and his wife Mary. On February 10, 1676, for example, Hinckley, on colony business in Boston, wrote to his "Dear Love," safe at home in Barnstable on Cape Cod, of the war's latest turns, but also of how much he missed her: "I long to be with thee; but it cannot yet be.... Meanwhile, I desire and hope God's gracious presence will be with thee, far better than mine, to support and carry thee through any present troubles and difficulties. Continue prayers for him that cannot forget thee, but remain[s], thine."[112]

Of concern to Penelope, too, at this time would have been the well-being of other family members and friends. News would have arrived sporadically, and rumors abounded. An October 1675 letter written by Mary Herendean Pray of Providence, Rhode Island, to Captain James Oliver of Boston, for example, reflects the insufficiency and unreliability of certain wartime reports. Mary Pray had received word that "Captain [Samuel] Mosley an[d] 3 hundred men with him are al cut ofe," but that defeat did not happen. She had also heard that "the Indians purpose was this winter to come down in the night...and feir [fire] our town." Pray had a very personal stake in the conflict, as her two sons were involved—she asked Captain Oliver to send her two "cutlashes [cutlasses] an[d] belts" for them—but she was also alarmed about the fate of New England. "Sir, if a spe[e]dy dispach be not, provision will be so scers [scarce] that men wil not be able to goe out and fight, and then the contery will be lost."[113]

Penelope's fears about the war's impact on friends and relatives were well founded, as whole communities were laid waste. As Josiah Cotton described it, the war was "attended with the...burning of houses, the murdering of men, women, and children; desolation of towns and settlements; tedious and terrible captivities, and continual fears and dangers."[114] (*The Sovereignty and Goodness of God,* a narrative written by Mary Rowlandson of Lancaster,

Massachusetts, about enduring one of these "terrible captivities," became a bestseller after the war.)

For Northeastern Native tribes, the war caused untold suffering. Traditional homelands were lost forever, communities were scattered, and families torn apart. The hard line that Josiah and the Plymouth government took against those who were even suspected of siding with Metacom included selling many Native peoples into the brutal slave system of the West Indies. During the war, noncombatants as well as warriors were killed. The December 1675 Rhode Island engagement known as "the Great Swamp Fight" in the Narragansett Indian country ended with the burning of Native homes sheltering hundreds of women and children. This devastating atrocity was celebrated by the colonists as a victory.[115]

Even the neutral "praying Indians"—Native peoples who had converted to Christianity—were punished for the war. Great numbers were interned on Boston's harbor islands, where many perished from exposure, illness, and starvation. Although the exact number of those detained is unknown, it has been estimated at 500 to 1,100, and is possibly much higher.[116]

Despite the destruction wreaked on Native communities during and as a result of King Philip's War, Indigenous peoples managed to survive and retain their culture and traditional ways. Although official records of the time depict defeated and subjugated Native peoples, the material evidence demonstrates a continued vitality and strength in their communities, even in a place that had witnessed such horrific loss as Rhode Island's Great Swamp. Nearby archaeological excavations have unearthed Native-made stone tools and shards of colonial glass refashioned into Native implements. These small relics reveal an ongoing Narragansett presence in the area, a sustained ability to adapt colonial objects to meet Native needs, and an enduring connection to hereditary lands.[117]

Chapter 6
LOSS

The killing of Metacom by colonial forces in August 1676 brought the war in Southeastern New England to an end. Following many months of anxious waiting, Penelope was finally reunited with Josiah in Marshfield. She turned her attention to restoring her household and family to as much normalcy as possible. Reconnecting with friends and neighbors, she was able to discover details of how other families had fared during her absence. While both her home and the town of Marshfield had been spared, Plymouth Colony had been rocked to its core, suffering great loss of life, property damage, and financial reversal. Court records mention wounded soldiers and widowed women applying for relief long after the war's close. It would take years for the colony to fully recover and come to terms with the trauma.

Given the war's devastation, Josiah was sensitive to the way its causes were interpreted. In July 1675, he had written to Massachusetts Bay Governor Leverett that "a friend in Boston" had informed him that "some are pleased to sensure us highly as if wee had ungroundedly enterprized this warr." Although this disturbed him, he was not overly concerned, as he believed "the enemie was long in armes before wee fired, allarmed our people, after which we courted [Metacom] by an amicable letter to dismiss his strangers [Indians from other parts], lay down armes, and bee quiet, uppon which hee profanely [attacked] our people by severall hostill acts."[118] Josiah reaffirmed and expanded on these rationales in a "Breiff Narrative of the Begining and Progresse of the P[re]sent Trouble between Us and the Indians; Takeing Its Rise in the Collonie of New Plymouth," which he composed in the fall of 1675 with Assistant Governor Thomas Hinckley.

After the war, several observers rushed to get their accounts into print. They knew their narratives would be read in England as well as America, and wanted to offer an interpretation of the conflict that would not reflect poorly on New England. Chief among these were Rev. William Hubbard of Ipswich, Massachusetts, and the esteemed Puritan divine Increase Mather (father to Rev. Cotton Mather, and step-brother of Plymouth minister John Cotton). Mather, whose *Brief History of the War with the Indians* (1676) interpreted the war as a scourge sent by God to punish New Englanders for their sinfulness, included Josiah and Thomas Hinckley's narrative in his history, as well as a letter written to him by Josiah on May 1, 1676. In the letter, Josiah continued to maintain the good intentions of Plymouth, stating that "the English did not possess one foot of Land in this Colony, but what was fairly obtained by honest purchase of the Indian Proprietors: Nay, because some of our people are of a covetous disposition, and the Indians are in their Streits easily prevailed with to part with their Lands, we first made a Law that none should purchase or receive of gift any Land of the Indians, without the knowledge and allowance of our Court." He also argued that, "if at any time [Native peoples] have brought complaints before us, they have had justice impartial and speedily, so that our own people have frequently complained, that we erred on the other hand in shewing them overmuch favour." In the end, Josiah seems to have interpreted the war partly as a sign of God's displeasure of the colonists' failure to convert more Native peoples to Christianity: "we must own that God is just and hath punished us far less than our iniquityes have deserved; yea just in using as a Rod, whose enlightning and Conversion we have not endeavoured as we might & should have done, but on the contrary have taught them new sins that they knew not."[119]

Penelope's own attempts to reclaim her life following the war included helping Josiah with aspects of his work. High on the agenda was the need to restore his reputation with the British monarch. King Charles II was angry that colonial-Native relations had declined to the point where they had erupted in warfare, and demanded an explanation for the hostilities. Josiah responded by drafting a report in which he asserted that Plymouth's late "troubles occasioned by the rebellion of our neighboring Sachems[,] or Indian Princes[,] and their people and allies" had not been "provoked." Josiah and Penelope made plans for Penelope's brother Waldegrave, then living at the family home Ferriers back in England, to deliver the report to court along with a war prize: "the best of the spoils of the ornaments and treasure of Sachem Philip, the grand rebel, being…his crown…and two belts of [the Natives'] own making of their gold and silver." Waldegrave, however, proved unworthy of this trust, as the king never received the items or Josiah's letter. In an enduring mystery, Metacom's war regalia remains lost to this day. [120]

In the coming years, as Great Britain attempted to exert more direct political and economic control over the colonies, Penelope helped Josiah develop a positive personal relationship with the king's emissary, Edward Randolph (1632–1703). Massachusetts Bay was openly defiant of what they perceived as Randolph's intrusion, but Josiah, in an attempt to help preserve Plymouth Colony's independence, sought a more conciliatory approach.

Unlike Massachusetts, Plymouth was never awarded a charter, or official title to its lands, from the Crown. Although the colony had made repeated efforts over the decades to obtain one, it had felt fairly secure during the years when Parliament and Oliver Cromwell were in power. After the restoration of the monarchy in 1660, however, Charles II made it clear he would establish more personal authority over the American colonies. Josiah recognized the precariousness of Plymouth's position, and sought to be as obliging to the British government as possible.[121]

Josiah and Penelope hosted Randolph at their home on more than one occasion, and Randolph was suitably impressed with the charms of their hospitality. At one point he stayed with the couple for a whole "sevennight." These efforts bore results in the Crown's granting to Plymouth Colony Metacom's former homeland of Mount Hope, a region "seven thousand acres, more or less," in recognition of its "loyalty and good conduct" in the war, by which it was the "happy instruments to enlarge [England's] dominion." Josiah received gratifying communications recognizing his "great merit and eminency expressed on all occasions where the interest of his majesty and his subjects [were] concerned," and acknowledging that "his majesty remain[ed] very well satisfied with [Josiah's] particular services, and with the dutifulness and loyal expressions of [Plymouth] Colony."[122]

As Josiah continued to conduct political duties from their home, Penelope remained closely attuned to colony affairs. As time passed, their daughter Elizabeth was able to assume some of Penelope's social duties and even occasionally help Josiah with administrative tasks. In 1679, for example, when Elizabeth was fifteen, he enlisted her to witness a property transaction involving a Duxbury neighbor. Elizabeth's signature on the deed is large and blocky, not like her mother's elegant script. But it is clearly written, and has much to recommend it over the mark of the other witness, Sarah Gray (likely the sister of Penelope's companion Elizabeth), who signed with an "X." (Many people who were able to read during this period could not sign their names, so "marks" were recognized as valid and as binding as a signature.)[123]

The war had taken a great toll on Josiah's health. Although in the decade of the 1670s he was only in his forties, he had not been well for some time. References to his illnesses pop up periodically: a 1673 letter from physician (and blacksmith) William Avery of Dedham prescribed remedies for Josiah's "nephritic disorder" (or inflammation of the kidneys). By 1676 Josiah had had to pass military command of the United Colonies' forces to Captain Benjamin Church. A 1677 letter from Rev. Samuel Arnold of Marshfield to Rev. John Cotton of Plymouth expressed Arnold's hope that Josiah was "mending." [124]

The days leading up to Josiah's death in 1680 were not pleasant ones. Boston diarist Samuel Sewall recorded that Josiah had suffered with "sore Pain with the Gout and Griping. His flesh was opened to the bone on's [on his] leggs before he dyed." [125] Penelope apparently did everything in her power to ease Josiah's suffering, administering some of the homemade remedies all housewives typically kept on hand—fragments of drug pots were found in the archaeological excavations—and also obtaining the best available medical help. (It is not known exactly which physicians tended to Josiah, but when Penelope's son Isaac was "dangerously sick" in 1695, she called on James Bailey, a physician and minister of Harvard's class of 1669.) The inventory taken following Josiah's death notes that his medical care may have cost as much as £20. [126]

Josiah's legacy as governor has largely been regarded by historians as a negative one. It is widely perceived that his lack of diplomacy and questionable efforts to acquire Indian lands helped ignite King Philip's War. His tactics for suppressing Native peoples during the war could be brutal. Yet as governor, he did implement some liberal policies, helping to establish the colony's first school and re-instituting the civil rights of individuals who had been disenfranchised by the previous governor for supporting Quakers. By his peers, he was widely esteemed; in fact, the Plymouth government paid £40 toward his funeral expenses "as a testimoniall of the collonies indeared love and affection unto him." [127]

Following Josiah's death, he was memorialized in numerous tributes. An oration held at the next Harvard commencement "much lamented" his passing. The "Bereaved and distressed" Thomas Hinckley, who succeeded Josiah as governor, wrote that, in addition to being a "Great ornament and crown to the colony," he had been "Large [in] wisdom, love, and friendly courtesy[,] Noble and free…full of charity." Reverend William Witherell of neighboring Scituate declared that "For kind behaviour [he was] lov'd by all[,] that knew him…both great and small;…Compassion lodg'd within his breast; To [the] poore ope'[n] were heart[,] hand[,] and chest." Rev. Josiah Cotton lauded him as "a worthy and well-accomplished gentleman, deservedly beloved by the people, being a true friend to their just liberties, generous, facetious, affable, and sincere, qualities incident to the family." If even a small fraction of these accolades were true, there was another side to his personality, with redeeming characteristics. This, perhaps, was the person Penelope knew. [128]

No writings remain to tell us whether the marriage of Josiah and Penelope had been a romantic one, but a few clues hint that it had been a union based on respect and strong affection. In his will, Josiah appointed Penelope the sole executrix of his estate, all of which was to be left to her "for her support and lively hood And for the bringing up of [their] children." Widows during this period were typically given a third of their husband's property for use during their lifetime or until they remarried; Penelope was given discretion over the entire estate up until the time her son Isaac turned twenty-one, at which point he would inherit half. Property and heritage were extremely important to Josiah, yet he entrusted Penelope with the option of selling up to half of the Marshfield acreage if she needed it for the family's "support and comfort" and other lands for "necessary occasions as she may see cause."[129]

No accounts of Josiah's funeral appear to have survived (other than Plymouth Colony Secretary Nathaniel Morton's comment that he was sorry to have missed it due to illness and the "badness of the weather"), but we can be sure it was a well-attended occasion marked by elaborate ceremony. Contemporary funerals of governors customarily included large processions and the carrying of military armor symbolizing the deceased's former status as "a gentleman and a protector of the people." Although the Puritans were known for rejecting many of the burial rituals of both the Catholic Church and Church of England—early funerals were simple burials lacking official religious observance—as the seventeenth century progressed, funerals became increasingly extravagant. This was particularly true for the elite, who began distributing gloves, scarves, and rings as gifts but also as manifestations of the deceased's wealth. Because funerals had been stripped of most of their religious aspects, they took on an important social dimension.[130]

Penelope is believed to have commemorated the loss of Josiah by commissioning a "mourning" ring by Boston gold- and silversmith John Coney. This particular small-sized ring, which carries one of Coney's marks, was an especially high-style version (*fig. 20*). Fashioned of gold and embellished with a design of flowers and vines, it features a hollow center enclosing a lock of what is presumably Josiah's hair. Unusual for the time, the ring does not carry Josiah's name, initials, or any type of inscription. Given the lack of accompanying documentation, we must be cautious about definitively attributing ownership to Penelope.[131]

We do know Penelope had a difficult time with Josiah's passing. The letter she received after his death from Nathaniel Morton (directed to his "Most

Respected Christian friend Mistress Winslow") attests to her deep sadness. Morton tried to console her with the fact that Josiah had "died in his bed under [her] Inspection[,] care[,] and diligence and the manifestation of [her] utmost and best Endeavours [she] could doe for his recovery," rather than on the battlefield. He also provided words of spiritual comfort that might "somewhat alleviate [her] grief," which he had "heard hath prevailed much" on her. Pointing out that Josiah was no longer suffering, that he was in a better place, and that although she had lost "the society of a precious husband," the Lord would fill that role by watching over her and her family, Morton also asked Penelope "to consider that nothing hath befallen [her], in respect of [her] great and sore loss[,] but what hath and may befall the best of Gods saints." He closed by calling on the words of Rev. John Robinson, the Pilgrims' former pastor in Holland, who "saith he we are not to mourn for the death of our Christian friends…either in regard of them or of ourselves;…because such as are asleep with Jesus God will [enter]…a more glorious life;…but we should take occasion by their deaths to love the world the less out of which they are taken; and heaven the more whither they are gone before us; and where we shall ever enjoy them." [132]

Letters such as Morton's urging the bereaved to rely on faith were common at the time; in 1684, for example, Plymouth minister John Cotton counseled then-Plymouth Colony First Lady Mary Hinckley after the death of a grandchild: "hearing that you are deeply dejected under the late bereaving stroake of Gods hand in your family, I cannot but in Conscience of my duty to God & in compassion to you,…speake a few words that may by divine blessing tend to allay that excessive greife that hath taken hold of you." Following the 1647 death of Governor John Winthrop's wife Margaret, Penelope's own father had written to sympathize in "the loss of [his] deare yolk fellow, whom the Lord hath taken to himself," but also advised, "though your own and the country's loss therein be very great, yet our comfort is when the streams fail we may go to the fountain." [133]

Nathaniel Morton's letter's reference to a spiritual crisis Penelope had previously undergone urged her to recall "former experiences of the Goodnes[s] of God" towards her when she was "in Great affliction of mind som[e] years since." "God brought you through those difficulties," he reminded her, "Now [c]all to mind what God did then for you and Improve it in this pr[e]sent sad affliction." An undated letter from Morton to Penelope addressing her as his "Esteemed Christian friend" was written in response to that experience, providing her with counsel and biblical passages that might help vanquish her "sad state." Admitting that he did not have the extent of "knowledge, faith and Christian experience" of more qualified individuals, such as ministers and elders, Morton noted that he nevertheless felt compelled to offer some words of encouragement because of his own personal experience. "Having been under desertion of spirit, and still often am, I myself can the better g[u]ess at them…"[134]

While Penelope's response to Morton, if any, has not survived, his letter alone offers invaluable insight into her interior life. It appears that the roots of her crisis—while likely exacerbated by the traumas of King Philip's War—lay in her fears that she was not among the saved. According to Puritan belief, individuals were predestined for either salvation or damnation. There was no way of knowing the ultimate fate of one's soul, but chances for salvation were far better for those who had undergone a "conversion"— the conviction that one had received God's grace and was reborn in faith. This experience, which was necessary for formal church membership, provided some reassurance to counter the deep anxiety that afflicted many devout Puritans.

Morton's letter perceived that "Sathan" was "assault[ing] & troubl[ing] [Penelope's] soul," and recognized that in her "present distresse," she had judged herself "lost and undone" and wondered whether she would be saved. Attempting to reassure her of God's mercy, he also anticipated any further self-questioning. "Oh the…compassion that is in our gracious God to poor mourning sinners. But the soul will, still further, object, I have been taught that whosoever shall be saved are only such as are elected [members of the "elect"], and are destined to eternal life; but I know not that I am within the electing love of God. I feare I am not…. For if I find that except I am born again, I cannot see the kingdom of God…But I know not whether I have any truth of grace or noe." The answer, he advised, lay in faith: "If you have faith, then you are really sanctified, born again."[135]

Morton was confident that Penelope would find relief should she heed his counsel: "sometimes by weak & inconsiderable means [such, as he noted, his own attempts] God is pleased to improve to bring about his gracious and glorious ends." He also consoled her with the fact that she was not the only one with such concerns: "Be assured that your condition is not singular, and that nothing hath befallen you respecting your present desertion, but that which is ordinary and common to the best of saints."[136]

Penelope certainly was not alone in being apprehensive about her spiritual future; Puritan writings brim with such uneasiness. Her own sister Jemima had evidently gone through a similar trial, as attested to by Rev. Ralph

Josselin's diary entry about encouraging her to "rowle her soule on god in christ" when she had been "under feares." (Interestingly, at the time of Herbert Pelham's death in 1674, Josselin noted in his diary that Herbert had been "a choice Saint, but faultie in his children. he minded them not to counsell them in sickness"—suggesting that Herbert had not been able to provide the necessary guidance to Jemima during the illness that accompanied her crisis.)[137] Penelope herself appears to have found support within her community. Morton references the "kind" offices on her behalf of the ministers and elders, as well as the "prayers of the saints," her fellow Puritans.

Penelope clearly found Morton's words comforting, as she preserved his letter for the rest of her life. Surviving church records do not indicate whether she ever became a full church member, but we do know she eventually moved beyond her "sad state."

This crucial episode in Penelope's life presents another aspect to her character; balancing the image of wealth, power, and self-confidence projected by much of the surviving physical evidence with proof of introspection, vulnerability, and self-doubt. A counterpoint to her external displays of identity, her spiritual struggles reveal further nuances in her experience, and additional depths to her personality.

Chapter 7
"THE ENJOYMENT OF HER DUE PROPORTION"

Penelope lost Josiah at the relatively young age of forty-seven; given average life expectancies for Plymouth Colony at that time, she could have expected to live to around seventy.[138] The "widdow[']s bed" referenced in the probate inventory taken following Josiah's death starkly symbolizes the specter of loneliness that may have shadowed her later years. She never remarried.

Ultimately, Penelope came to terms with her situation as a widow and managed to carry a significant load of financial and familial responsibility. Of course, she had previously done so during the many years Josiah had traveled on colony and military business, and evidently had been so successful that Josiah had appointed her the sole executrix of his estate. She also had recourse to three advisers Josiah had selected should she need outside counsel: her brother-in-law George Corwin; Corwin's son-in-law, merchant Peter Sergeant; and Josiah's cousin, Nathaniel Winslow of Marshfield.

One of Penelope's most important obligations following Josiah's death was continuing the education of her children, Elizabeth and Isaac, then sixteen and nine. (Josiah had specified in his will that he wished both of his children to be given a good education, yet he also observed the distinction that this would vary "according to their sex.") Elizabeth's future in particular needed tending to, as she was approaching marriageable age. Penelope, as one of the most educated women in the area, likely herself continued Elizabeth's schooling, as well as teaching her about running a household. She also would have sent Elizabeth on visits to her sister-in-law Elizabeth Corwin in Salem or her aunt Penelope Bellingham in Boston to widen her social circle and introduce her to eligible bachelors. These efforts evidently came to fruition when, four years after Josiah's death, Elizabeth married the recently widowed Stephen Burton.

A wealthy merchant who is rumored to have emigrated from London and attended Oxford, Burton first appears in the Boston records around 1670. After the end of King Philip's War, he and three other investors purchased Mount Hope from Plymouth Colony. In 1681, they were authorized to establish the town of Bristol, now part of Rhode Island, which is where he and Elizabeth married in September 1684.[139] (Burton's first wife, Abigail Brenton, herself had been the daughter of a colonial governor, William Brenton of Rhode Island.)

Burton's wealth would have ensured Elizabeth a comfortable lifestyle. Nevertheless, she faced many challenges. Being far from family and friends, she had to make new connections. Upon her marriage, she became stepmother to Stephen's two young children, seven-year-old Stephen junior (born 1677) and four-year-old Martha (born 1680). Her own first child, a daughter named Penelope born in 1686, did not live long.

Beginning in 1685, Stephen served for several years as a representative from Bristol to the Plymouth General Court. If Elizabeth was prevented by childcare duties from traveling with him to Plymouth, she would have spent frequent intervals on her own. Just a few years into her marriage, Stephen became ill. A note in the Bristol County probate records mentions that for a "considerable time before his death" in July 1693, he had been troubled with "some Distemper in his head." The condition had apparently been quite serious, as it caused him to become "very remiss in Recording and Keeping the records of the court" in his role as Bristol County clerk.[140]

By the time of Stephen's death, Elizabeth had two additional children, a daughter, Elizabeth, about four, and a four-month-old son, Thomas. Rather than staying in Bristol, she chose to rejoin Penelope in Marshfield. Thereafter she occasionally sold parcels of the land she had inherited from Stephen. Several surviving deeds carry her signature and her seal.[141]

✶ ✶ ✶ ✶ ✶

Penelope's son Isaac, at nine years old, was at a much earlier stage of his education at the time of his father's death. A few years previously, he, like Elizabeth, when young, may have attended one of Plymouth's local "dame schools"—so called because they were run by women in their homes. Dame schools were in effect from Plymouth's early years; the 1633 will of Dr. Samuel Fuller, for example, specified that both his son and daughter should be taught by "mrs Heeks." As Isaac grew older, he likely continued his studies with a local minister, as did other boys from well-to-do homes. Plymouth's Rev. John Cotton, for instance, sent his sons to study with Rev. Ichabod Wiswall of nearby Duxbury and also with Boston clergymen.[142]

Surprisingly, unlike many of his peers and breaking with family tradition, Isaac did not attend Harvard. It is highly likely he wanted to remain in Marshfield to oversee the property that would eventually become his, and to help his mother with the running of it. In any case, his education was sufficiently extensive to qualify him for his later work as a probate court and Inferior Court of Common Pleas judge (and later as the latter court's chief justice), and as president of the Council of the Province of Massachusetts Bay.

Like his father before him, Isaac also became a military man, commissioned as a colonel in the Massachusetts militia in 1715.

Penelope cared for the older generation as well as the younger, making a home for her aging aunt Elizabeth Pelham. A surviving trunk bearing the initials "EP" said to have descended through the family may have belonged to Elizabeth Pelham. If so, it would testify to the rather peripatetic nature of her life. Although Elizabeth appears to have been welcomed into the households of family members such as Penelope, as an unmarried woman she was left in the position of never having had a home of her own. (Of resilient stock, Elizabeth would ultimately outlive Penelope by three years, dying in the "84th year of [her] age" in 1706; *fig. 22*.)[143]

In 1685, Penelope decided to sell a lot of land in Little Compton (formerly the lands of the Sakonnet tribe, now part of Rhode Island) for the large sum of £140, citing her "good Right[,] full power[,] and lawful authority" to do so. And in 1688 she distributed a substantial amount of land in Bristol County to her then-married daughter Elizabeth. The deeds transferring this property both carry Penelope's personal seal, an emblem of her status and authority.[144]

Window leads dating from around 1683 found on the Winslow property reveal that Penelope continued to update her home.[145] Within her community, she maintained a position of respect as the governor's widow and a woman of property and genteel lineage, being addressed as "Madam." She also enjoyed a great deal of personal autonomy.

In the decades following Josiah's death, Plymouth Colony continued to evolve. With the seizure of Native lands and the expansion of settlement following King Philip's War, the colony grew to encompass a territory that included all of Southeastern Massachusetts and extended west to what is now Rhode Island. As a result of this growth, in 1685 the colony was divided into three counties: Plymouth, Barnstable on Cape Cod, and Bristol. (The population of the colony remained low; only around 10,000 by 1690.)[146]

Changes were afoot on a larger scale, too, as King Charles II and, after his death in 1685, his brother King James II worked to exert greater control over the New England colonies. In 1684, Charles had revoked the Massachusetts charter for noncompliance with his policies, including the Navigation Acts restricting international trade. In 1686, James consolidated the colonies of Plymouth, Massachusetts, Connecticut, New Hampshire, Maine, Rhode Island, and later New Jersey and New York, into the Dominion of New

England, under the rule of a royally appointed governor, Sir Edmund Andros, and council. Political self-representation was curtailed and new taxes imposed, to the colonists' deep distress. Adding insult to injury in the eyes of Puritan New Englanders was James' Catholic faith.

James' authoritarian policies and religious views were also widely opposed in England, and arrangements were made for him to be replaced with his daughter Mary and her husband, the Protestant William of Orange. What became known as the "Glorious Revolution" took place in late 1688; the following April, Josiah's cousin John Winslow arrived in Boston from Barbados with the news. Before even receiving official confirmation of the shift in government, Bostonians imprisoned Andros and his supporters. The Dominion was officially dissolved by William and Mary later that year. In Plymouth, Thomas Hinckley resumed the governorship.

In the Dominion's aftermath, Plymouth pursued efforts to maintain its independence, pleading its case with the British government. Yet it did not have the means, or seemingly the will, to fight for a charter. In the midst of a new war with the Indians on the northern frontier (King William's War 1688–1697, the first of a series known as the French and Indian Wars occurring intermittently 1688–1763) and a changing political climate, these attempts proved to no avail. Ultimately, the British government conveyed Plymouth (and Maine) to Massachusetts in its new charter of 1691. The transition was made in 1692.

Both Plymouth and Massachusetts lost representative government and the ability to shape their societies to reflect their religious beliefs with the new Massachusetts charter, which called for a royally appointed governor with expanded powers. Freedom of worship, which most Puritans had steadfastly opposed, was awarded to other Protestant denominations, and church membership was not required for voting privileges, counter to earlier Massachusetts Bay (but not Plymouth) law. The undermining of colonial authority created tensions between New England and Great Britain that would eventually lead to the fight for American independence. In just three generations, the holy experiment of creating a unique, godly "city on a hill" envisioned by the Puritan settlers had come to an end.[147]

✶ ✶ ✶ ✶ ✶

Given Penelope's commitment to the Puritan way, and her deep connection to Plymouth Colony's former government, she may have viewed Plymouth and Massachusetts's loss of self-determination with sadness. On a personal level, she never stopped being a proud and fierce protector of her own rights. Years before her father Herbert's death in 1674,[148] she accidentally discovered that she had never received a gift of £450 that her maternal grandfather, Thomas Waldegrave, had entrusted Herbert to make to each of his children after certain parcels of land had been sold. Over the years, Penelope repeatedly tried to acquire the distribution, and before Josiah's death in 1680 they had made arrangements with a London lawyer to work on their behalf. By this time, the funds were under the jurisdiction of Penelope's brother Waldegrave, who was executor of their late father's estate. A deposition Penelope submitted in 1683 expresses the hurt and outrage she felt at her father and brother's failure to pass along the bequest. Because it is one of the few chances we have to hear Penelope's voice, it is worth quoting at some length:

> Your said orator having lived at the time of the making of the said deed [by Thomas Waldegrave] and ever since in New England[,] was for a long time wholly ignorant of what her said grandfather did in the premises and since she came to the knowledge of the same she and her said husband Josiah Winslow esquire have often demanded the said sum of Herbert Pelham the father of your said orator[,] who on pretence of the right of his wife or on some other pretence entered into and enjoyed the said lands during his life[,] the said trustees not minding to perform the said trust. And your said orator further showeth…that Waldgrave Pelham esquire son and heir of the said Herbert is in the possession of the said lands claiming the same by descent or by some other title…and now wholly denies to pay to your said orator the sum or sums due to your said orator as aforesaid[,] although the said Waldgrave Pelham…did often persuade and advise the said Herbert to pay the same as what was in equity due to your said [orator] by virtue of the said deeds[,] but the said Herbert Pelham combining and confederating together with divers other persons unknown to your said orator…to defraud your said orator of the premises….

Penelope concluded by asking the court to subpoena her brother, "to answer the premises and further to stand to and abide such further order and directions therein as to Your Lordship shall seem most meet."[149]

It appears that Penelope received some type of settlement as a result of her appeal. As she requested, Waldegrave did appear in court to present the inventory of Herbert Pelham's estate, as well as his account as executor. But he proved inept at properly settling the estate, which was wracked by debts that Waldegrave himself added to, and never distributed the family's legacies in full. Penelope and her siblings—and her aunts Elizabeth Pelham and Penelope Pelham Bellingham—joined in pressing lawsuits. Decades later, they were still expecting a disbursement. As the Plymouth minister John Cotton wrote in a 1695 letter to his son Rowland, "I saw madam winslow & mris Pelham; Ned [Penelope's half-brother Edward] [is] well in o[ld]: E[ngland]: a 1000 pd & more is due to them with mris Bellingham, which they have reason to think he will bring them this summer." [150]

Penelope's legal battles eventually came to include her half-brother Edward, who by 1702 had moved to Newport and married Freelove Arnold, the daughter of former Rhode Island governor Benedict Arnold (who may have been an ancestor of the famous American Revolutionary War traitor of the same name). That year Edward laid claim to 400 acres that in 1648 had been granted by the Massachusetts General Court to Herbert Pelham, along with 400 acres that had been given to the heirs of Penelope's grandfather Thomas Waldegrave. In 1703, Penelope, at the age of seventy, sent a remarkable petition to Massachusetts Governor Joseph Dudley and his council to state her own claim (*fig. 21*). (Dudley was well known to her, as during Josiah's lifetime he had "been very often received...at [their] house.") [151]

Although her now-adult son Isaac, who in 1703 joined the Massachusetts governor's council, likely advised her on the petition, the tone and language appear to be her own. Laying out the facts of the case, she noted that she, as well as Edward, was a deserving heir of Herbert Pelham, but that Edward had "no Right at all" to the lands of Thomas Waldegrave, as he was completely unrelated to him (as the son of Penelope's stepmother Elizabeth Harlakenden). Assigning the land to Edward, she argued, would be "very Injurious and a great wrong to your petitioner to whome of right ye greatest part of s[ai]d lands doth appertain." She requested that when the 800 acres were laid out, she "not be debarred of her just Rights of and in ye same but that...she may come to ye Enjoyment of her due proportion": 600 acres. [152]

Penelope was clearly stung by what appears to have been Edward's deception in representing himself as a legitimate heir of Thomas Waldegrave and as the only local heir of Herbert Pelham. His subterfuge must have particularly pained her since she had taken him into her home when as a young man he had first come to New England, and following on the heels of her father and brother Waldegrave's failure to provide her proper inheritance. [153] Although these men were the ones who carried the family name, Penelope deeply believed in her own "just Rights" as a Pelham and Waldegrave heir. Ultimately, her battle for the disputed land was largely settled in her favor, but not resolved until years after her death, which occurred just months after the submission of her petition.

Chapter 8
REMEMBRANCE

No description of Penelope's funeral appears to have survived, but it is to be hoped it was an occasion fitting to her status as a former Plymouth Colony First Lady: a tribute to the service she had provided and the personal sacrifices she had made. Over the course of Penelope's life, her personal history had become deeply intertwined with that of the former colony; she had prospered with it and suffered with it. With the colony's passing—and, earlier, with the death of Josiah—she had had to reinvent herself, establishing a new identity based on what she had accomplished and who she could yet become. In maintaining the property left to her by Josiah, raising her children to become productive and successful adults, returning the care her aunt Elizabeth had provided her with as a girl, and successfully claiming inheritances she was entitled to, she clearly met these challenges.

Following Penelope's death, her daughter Elizabeth Winslow Burton and Elizabeth's two children, Elizabeth and Thomas, continued to live in Marshfield. Surviving deeds indicate that by 1715 they were residents of nearby Duxbury. It is not known what happened to Penelope and Josiah's home, but it was no longer standing by early 1726, as that year Penelope's son Isaac referred to the site in a deed as "[where] the Old House formerly stood."[154]

Penelope's daughter Elizabeth never remarried, perhaps enjoying the freedom that came from being a wealthy widow. However, one detail complicates the image of Elizabeth as a leisured gentlewoman: in 1713, and again in 1719, the Plymouth Court of Sessions and Pleas awarded a retail liquor license to a "Mistress" Elizabeth Burton. This does not mean Elizabeth was running a tavern, but that she was able to earn income from sales of alcohol. Although other high-status women and men—with "Mistress" and "Esq." attached to their name—held these licenses in Plymouth, for Elizabeth to seek an economic opportunity of this type was certainly a break with family tradition.[155]

Elizabeth remained close with her children, eventually moving with them from Duxbury to Pembroke. She died in 1735, having lived into her early seventies. Her gravestone, like that of her aunt Elizabeth Pelham, bears the common symbol of the Puritan death's head, but rendered more fancifully (*fig. 23*). With its heart-shaped mouth and wavy hair, it embodies a "softening" of ideas about the afterlife resulting from the decline in Puritan orthodoxy. In the former Plymouth Colony, one of the visual ways in which this religious transformation was expressed was through a stylistic transition in gravestone art.[156]

Elizabeth Winslow Burton's daughter Elizabeth never married. A nineteenth-century chronicler noted of her that, "marvellous stories [were] told of the elegance of her personal belongings, one tradition being that she had a 'quart measure of jewels,' and many magnificent dresses." Apparently Penelope's granddaughter had inherited her taste for fine clothing. Some of Elizabeth's belongings, in fact, may have been passed down from her grandmother. Perhaps seeing her mother and grandmother's independence as single women influenced Elizabeth's own decision not to marry; she inherited property from her father so had resources at her disposal. In 1722 she sold these lands to her brother Thomas for the hefty sum of £400.[157]

Elizabeth Winslow Burton's son Thomas lived a quieter life than those of his Winslow male ancestors. He did not pursue high public office or military leadership. Described by an early twentieth-century local historian as a man "of high family and much learning," he worked as a schoolteacher and as Pembroke's town clerk. After marrying in his late twenties, he and his wife, the former Alice Wadsworth, had four daughters, one of whom they named Penelope.[158]

Penelope's son Isaac became a leading figure in the new Plymouth County, serving in military and judicial roles. In 1700, when he was almost thirty, Isaac married Sarah Wensley of Boston in a service performed by the eminent Cotton Mather. (An evocative portrait of Sarah's mother, Elizabeth Paddy Wensley (1641–1711), painted by an unknown Boston artist circa 1670–1680, hangs in Pilgrim Hall Museum.)

Like Penelope, Isaac's wife Sarah was an educated and self-confident woman. In a 1746 letter written by Sarah and Isaac's son Edward to his brother John, Edward noted that, although John's son Pelham was still with Edward in Boston, "under the Tuition of Mr Ward," John's son Isaac "remain[ed] with his grandmother at Marshfield[,]who thinks She can teach as well as anyone."[159]

Around the time of Isaac's marriage to Sarah, he built a "mansion house" near the site of Penelope's home. This house still stands. Although it has been enlarged over the years, it still maintains many of its early features, including original fireplaces, a dairy and pantry, molded paneling, decorative ceiling painting, and an ornamentally turned staircase. It has been speculated that the rear ell of the house may come from an earlier dwelling —perhaps the home of Edward and Susanna or Josiah and Penelope.[160]

Isaac and Sarah had six children together. Two sons, Josiah and John, who were born before Penelope's death, would follow in the male Winslow tradition of military service. Josiah, a Harvard graduate, was killed as a young man during a skirmish with Natives while leading an expedition in Maine in 1724. His small group included some "friendly Indians" who were known to him from his youth. After Josiah's death, Cotton Mather wrote a memorial sermon in his honor.[161]

Josiah's brother, General John Winslow, who inherited the family estate, is best known for having led the 1755 expulsion of Acadians from Nova Scotia. A sword that is believed to have belonged to him is housed at Pilgrim Hall Museum.

Isaac and Sarah's daughter Penelope was born the year after her namesake grandmother's death. She would become the mother of Revolutionary War Patriot General James Warren, who would marry the remarkable Mercy Otis, the political writer, playwright and historian. A surviving letter Isaac wrote to his daughter Penelope the year before her death in 1737, when she was in a "weak and low estate and condition," expressed his love for her and encouraged her to "cast [her] selfe into the arms of divine mercy thoroughly." Penelope Winslow Warren's 1707 Bible, in the collections of Pilgrim Hall Museum, may have been a comfort and support during her final days.[162]

Like his father Josiah before him, Isaac appears to have been regarded by his peers as an accomplished gentleman, a generous host, and an upright citizen. The Reverend Daniel Lewis observed that, "In stature, he was tall and rather gross [heavyset], but of noble aspect. He was [in] every way a gentleman, easy of access, facetious, of good, natural powers, given to hospitality, and universally beloved."[163] Like Josiah, too, Isaac felt a deep appreciation for the possessions that reinforced his status, identity, and authority.

In his 1736 will, Isaac gifted his "seal" ring, likely the one inherited from Josiah—and, perhaps, Edward before him—to his oldest son John. He gave his other rings and "Sword or rapiers" to his son Edward, and all his "arms and wearing apparel" to both sons. Among the most valuable of his personal possessions listed on the probate inventory taken following his death were his clothing, valued at £119; his books, valued at £99; his silver plate, valued at £155—and his slaves, valued at £250.[164]

Like many of his social peers, Isaac, and later some of his children, benefited from the use of slave labor. It not only helped support their livelihoods and properties, but served as a symbol of their wealth. Although slave ownership was not extensive in New England except in port cities like Boston, it increased during the eighteenth century as the "triangular" trade expanded. New England merchants sent ships to Africa to sell rum for slaves, who were taken to the West Indies to grow sugar, which was brought back to New England to make more rum. Slaves also arrived on these vessels.

Slavery in New England looked different from that in the South: except for some large farms in Rhode Island, most slaveowning households had only one or two slaves. Yet the system produced many of the same tragic effects, depriving individuals of their liberty; in many cases, their families; and in some instances, their lives. Only after the American Revolution, when African Americans successfully petitioned the courts for their freedom, was the institution declared illegal under the new state Massachusetts Constitution in 1783.

Isaac's inventory does not provide the names of his "servants," but the contemporary value of adult African slaves would equate the £250 value to roughly three or more individuals. We do know something about one of Isaac's slaves, a woman named Bettee who met a sad end. In October 1711, Bettee secretly gave birth to an infant whom she was afterwards accused of murdering. Her crime was compounded, it was said, by having afterwards concealed the body "so that it could not come to light whether that Child was born alive or not." The following spring, Bettee was "Arraigned[,] Tryed[,] & found Guilty of feloniously concealing the death of a Bastard Child," and that May was "Conve[ye]d from the Gaol in Plymouth unto the Place of execution…and hanged by the Neck untill…Dead."[165] Although she pled not guilty, she was convicted by a jury (a group of white men, they were certainly not her peers). Her story lives on in the court documents, but has not been preserved in the family records.

Some of Isaac's slaves may have passed down through his family. In addition, his son General John Winslow may have owned a man named Cato, and in the 1754 slave census John is listed as owning an adult female. This was possibly Jane, in connection with whom in 1788 the town of Marshfield filed suit against John's heirs so that they could get "clear of the Expenses" of maintaining her.[166]

Most memorably, Briton Hammon was one of the slaves owned by John. Hammon was the author of one of the first published American slave autobiographies, published in Boston in 1760, the *Narrative of the Uncommon Sufferings, and Surprizing Deliverance of Briton Hammon, a Negro Man,— Servant to General Winslow, of Marshfield, in New-England; Who Returned to Boston, After Having Been Absent Almost Thirteen Years. Containing an*

Account of the Many Hardships He Underwent from the Time He Left His Master's House, in the Year 1747, to the Time of His Return to Boston. Remarkably, after an absence of many years during which Hammon endured shipwreck, capture, and imprisonment in the course of making a sea voyage for John Winslow, Hammon encountered Winslow while on a ship bound back to Boston. He is believed to have re-entered his service, and his fate after that point is unknown.

Evidence of the slaves' residence at the Winslow house during the lifetimes of Isaac and his wife Sarah and their heirs is physically embedded in the home's history. A cowrie shell found in an archaeological excavation reflects an African or Indian Ocean origination. (Cowrie shells were used as currency, jewelry, and religious artifacts; one carved African cowrie shell recently discovered under the attic floorboards of the Newport Historical Society's Wanton-Lyman-Hazard House appears to have been part of an African "spirit bundle" placed there by a former slave.) The Winslow house's garret rooms housed both slaves and indentured Irish and English servants. A surviving game piece made from creamware reflects how the home's servants and slaves adapted the materials at hand to create opportunities for leisure and socialization.[167]

★ ★ ★ ★ ★

Penelope Pelham Winslow's pride in her aristocratic lineage and heritage— so strongly demonstrated in her quest to claim family inheritances—was also communicated to and replicated by Isaac and his children. Isaac's youngest son, Edward, born in 1714 and like his brother Josiah, a Harvard graduate, translated these values into loyalty to the British Crown during the American Revolution. Edward and his family, who included a daughter named Penelope, eventually abandoned their mansion house in Plymouth and fled to the British army in New York. (Their former residence now houses the headquarters of the General Society of Mayflower Descendants.) The family ultimately left New York for Nova Scotia.[168]

General John Winslow's sons Pelham and Isaac were Loyalists, too. Pelham was a Harvard graduate; when he entered college, his father had written to the president asking that Pelham's class rank, traditionally based on a student's father's civic rank rather than individual academic achievement, reflect the distinguished nature of the Winslow lineage ("it is Generaly allowed That The sons of the New England Cambridge are Placed according to the Degree of their ancestors[,] I have therefore put in My Pretensions for my Son"). Pelham eventually joined the British army, evacuating with them to Nova Scotia, but later returning to New York, where he died in 1783. His brother Isaac, a doctor who inherited the family home, was able to remain in Marshfield because of the value placed on his services. In 1778 he had treated approximately 300 patients inoculated with smallpox.[169]

As town historian Cynthia Hagar Krusell has pointed out, Marshfield was home to several other Tory families, wealthy landowners with distinguished backgrounds, many of whom held positions appointed by the British Crown. It is interesting to note that other branches of the Winslow family in Marshfield, descendants of Pilgrim Edward's brothers Kenelm and Josiah, who had not been as financially successful or politically active as Penelope and Josiah's family, sided with the Patriot cause.[170]

During the American Revolution, Penelope Pelham Winslow remained an important ancestor to her heirs because she could connect the family back to more aristocratic and socially prominent days. Her portrait and Josiah's served as powerful reminders of the family's former public significance. In 1776 one Loyalist Winslow descendant, Benjamin Marston, became particularly intrigued by Penelope and Josiah's union. The son of their son Isaac's daughter Elizabeth, Marston (who himself would seek sanctuary in Nova Scotia) recorded the following poem in his diary in December of that year. Although he wrote that the tribute had been composed anonymously in 1652 to commemorate Penelope and Josiah's marriage, it is quite possible he authored it himself. Notable among the lines is an expressed interest in the couple's progeny and their lineage: "Posterity is wedlock's crown/Issue to Nature adds renown/Ever may worthy issue bless their blood..../May they live long thus blessed & may each name/Wear the best Coat of Arms A Spotless fame."

PEACE & JOY

To the happy Nuptials of the much honoured
Mr. Josiah Winslow, and the truly
virtuous
Miss Penelope Pelham
Mr. Mrs.
Pure joys, clear fame & fortune fair
In all times crown this worthy Pair
Ever may they in virtue (spight
Of all repugnancies) shine bright
No rock can be their wreck no foe their fear
Set sail for heaven and do by virtue steer
Envy may then blow but not blast

In rudest Storms Firm Rocks stand fast
Love linked with virtue free from vice
Appears another paradise
Outward plenty mental peace
Holiness & Happiness
Preserve their joys & guide their way
Ever may reason rule passion obey
While reason's hand doth steer Love cannot stray
Posterity is wedlock's crown
Issue to Nature adds renown
Ever may worthy issue bless their blood
Nature produce them: fair Grace make them good
Love's true intentions make them ever prove
Sincerety to be soul of Love
Holiness make them Happiness to last
Like laurel which no Lightning can blast
Always may Goodness be their guide & Guard
Our Goodness Still finds safety for reward
May they live long thus blessed & may each name
Wear the best Coat of Arms A Spotless fame
Sir
May you since God a worthy wife did Give
With her still as a man of knowledge live
Mistress
May your responsive virtue ever prove
Obedience is no bondage where we love

—1652 author unknown[171]

As a result of the Revolution, Dr. Isaac Winslow suffered financial setbacks and became the Winslow home's last family owner. Following his death in 1822, the property was sold to pay off debts, subsequently passing through a series of owners (including neighbor and statesman Daniel Webster). In 1920, the Winslow House Association formed to preserve the property (*fig. 24*). The organization has been operating it as a historic house museum ever since.

Although anecdotal, a quote from an 1835 history of Plymouth tells us that, "The fact [was] well understood that many of this ancient family had been educated from infancy under the beguiling influence and favor of the Royal government."[172] The Winslows' pride in their British heritage and their high social rank and economic standing were threatened by Revolutionary rhetoric advocating for independence, equality, and liberty. The tidal wave of change brought by the American Revolution uprooted the English class system and social tradition of deference that had long been operating in New England. These developments challenged the Winslows' way of life and their deeply held sense of identity. The ways they chose to react to these changes had an impact that reverberated beyond their kinship connections and local community. As historians Julie Hardwick, Sarah M. S. Pearsall, and Karin Wulf have noted, American families' strategies for survival and advancement have often had ramifications that helped shape the Atlantic world.[173]

With American independence, the Winslow family lost their ancestral home and lands, most of their fortune, and their premier place in Massachusetts politics and the military—attributes that had defined them for generations. But they did succeed in holding onto treasured family relics, and continued to find meaning and significance in their heritage.

*****

Two final material objects play a role in Penelope Pelham Winslow's story. Marking her gravesite in the Winslow Burial Ground, located a short distance from her former home site, is a monument paying tribute to several members of her family. Unfortunately, it reduces Penelope's eventful life to a single role, identifying her merely as "Penelope ye Widdow of Gov[erno]^r Winslow."

Where her house once stood, a commemorative stone erected in the twentieth century reports that the spot had formerly been home to governors Edward and Josiah, completely disregarding the presence of Penelope and Susanna (and other members of the household). Like the Winslow gravestone, the marker is heavily symbolic of the erasure of women's history that has occurred over the centuries (*fig. 25*).

Despite Penelope's elite status and compelling life story, she ultimately shared the fate of most other Plymouth Colony women: her name has been mostly forgotten. In the centuries since her death in 1703, historians have spent little time considering her experiences or those of her female contemporaries, significant though they were. The one group who never stopped honoring her memory was her descendants: naming their daughters Penelope and their sons Pelham, preserving her belongings, and passing down stories that helped bring these possessions to life, even if some errors crept in along the way. Many of those who took the most active part in commemorating her life were women. As the traditional inheritors of personal property—the "moveables"—rather than real estate, women have often adopted the role of preservers of family heritage and heirlooms, but often, too, of important but overlooked pieces of the historical record.

An evocative collection of "things" survives to tell us about Penelope Pelham Winslow's life and times. Items such as her portrait and bodkin bring us physically closer to her, while artifacts of war, objects created by Native peoples, natural elements such as the African cowrie shell, and household goods acquired through European trade shed light on the social, political, and economic realities of her day. Combining traditional written sources with material culture allows us to recover the experiences of an elite individual like Penelope, but also those of more "ordinary" people. There are many more hidden, yet important, stories waiting to be told. It is up to us to find the ways to tell them.

Notes

1. Lisa Brooks, *Our Beloved Kin: A New History of King Philip's War* (New Haven: Yale University Press, 2018); *Wampanoag World: Patuxet to Plymouth,* Exhibition (February 24, 2018–April 7, 2019), Pilgrim Hall Museum, Plymouth, Mass.

2. John Demos, *A Little Commonwealth: Family Life in Plymouth Colony* (New York: Oxford University Press, 1970), 85.

3. Many *Mayflower* passenger lists note only eighteen adult women, discounting John and Katherine Carver's maidservant Dorothy (whose surname is as yet unknown), who would go on to marry fellow *Mayflower* passenger Francis Eaton.

4. Some of the above material was taken from *pathFOUNDERS: Women of Plymouth,* Exhibition (May 3, 2019–March 8, 2020), Pilgrim Hall Museum, Plymouth, Mass. curated by Donna Curtin and Michelle Marchetti Coughlin, with guest curator Linda Coombs.

5. Earlier work on Penelope Pelham Winslow has been conducted by Penelope Pelham Behrens, *Footnotes: A Biography of Penelope Pelham, 1633–1703* (Spentpenny Press, 1998); Peggy M. Baker, "A Touch of Purple: Penelope Winslow," https://www.pilgrimhall.org/pdf/Penelope_Pelham_Winslow.pdf; Karin J. Goldstein: "The Creation of a New England Gentry: The Winslows of Plymouth Colony" (master's thesis, University of Massachusetts Boston, 2001); and, most recently, Rebecca Fraser, *The Mayflower: The Voyage, the Families, and the Founding of America* (New York: St. Martin's Press, 2017). Baker's article contains detailed information about Penelope's royal connections.

6. A majority of the founders of Massachusetts Bay Colony came from the same general region as Penelope's family, East Anglia, which enhanced their cultural and kinship connections (David Hackett Fischer, *Albion's Seed: Four British Folkways in America* [New York: Oxford University Press, 1989], 31).

7. Penelope's reasons for remaining in Massachusetts while most of her family returned to England are unclear. Later events suggest that she may not have shared the most loving of relationships with her stepmother, the former Elizabeth Bosseville Harlakenden, whom her father married not long after arriving in New England.

8. For identification of Penelope's hair ornament as a pearl-trimmed hood, see Martha L. Finch, *Dissenting Bodies: Corporealities in Early New England* (New York: Columbia University Press, 2010), 114–115.

9. Based on Penelope's clothing and hairstyle, the circa 1651 date of her portrait is believed to be feasible by Royal Collections Curator of Paintings Anna Reynolds. Ms. Reynolds also notes that the 1650s are a difficult time for comparisons in British portraiture or fashion because of the scarcity of female portraits painted during the Commonwealth period (Anna Reynolds e-mail to Rebecca Fraser, January 21, 2014).

John Eliot's letter to Edward Winslow is dated "20t[h] of the 8[th month]. 1651" and is quoted in G. D. Scull, "Letters of the Rev. John Eliot, the Apostle to the Indians," *New England Historical and Genealogical Register* 36 (1882): 292.

10. *Fashion: The Definitive History of Costume and Style* (New York: Smithsonian/ DK Publishing, 2012), 125–126. The portrait of Princess Mary Stuart painted by Gerard van Honthorst is now at Britain's National Trust's Ashdown House.

11. Plymouth Colony had little in the way of sumptuary laws, but custom dictated dressing according to one's social class.

12. Finch, *Dissenting Bodies,* 107–116.

13. A recent excavation of the Robert Waterman homesite at Marshfield's municipal airport, which burned down circa 1643–1645, uncovered the earliest known European textiles in New England and included fragments of silk and silver galloon (Nathanial Crockett, "Burning Down the House! An Analysis of Carbonized Textiles from the Waterman Site, Marshfield, Massachusetts" [master's thesis, University of Rhode Island, 2016], 22–23).

14. In the early nineteenth century, the shoes were inherited by two brothers, Penelope's great-great-grandsons. In 1836, one of the brothers, seventy-eight-year-old Elkanah Watson, donated his shoe to Pilgrim Hall Museum. Watson was under the impression that the shoe had belonged to Penelope's mother-in-law Susanna, and wrote on a slip of paper still attached to its sole that it was his "earnest wish that a relick so ancient[,] so precious in the archives of New England, and so well authenticated, may be carefully transmitted to posterity." The other shoe descended with a note saying that it had been worn by Penelope at her marriage to Josiah. Pilgrim Hall Museum Catalog Record 147a; Behrens, *Footnotes: A Biography of Penelope Pelham,* i.

15. The likelihood of the shoes belonging to a man has been confirmed by fashion historian Kimberly Alexander, University of New Hampshire (e-mail message to author, March 12, 2018); Susan North, Curator of Fashion 1550–1800, Victoria and Albert Museum (e-mail message to author, March 5, 2018); and Rebecca Shawcross, Senior Shoe Curator, the Guildhall/Northampton Museums and Art Gallery (e-mail message to author, March 13, 2018).

16. The error about the shoes' ownership is understandable given the dramatic evolution in men's footwear that occurred in the centuries following the popularity of men's mules. Today, high heels carry cultural connotations of femininity, yet they were actually first worn by men. As Elizabeth Semmelhack points out in "Standing Tall: The Curious History of Men in Heels," high heels originated in Western Asia in the Middle Ages, perhaps around the time of the stirrup's introduction, and at the turn of the seventeenth century they began appearing in Western Europe. At that time they symbolized rugged masculinity due to their association with the Persian cavalry, then the largest in the world. High heels were eventually popularized by the French and English courts of Louis XIV and Charles II, and

thereafter became associated with political power and refinement. Women only started wearing high heels as the result of a 1630s trend incorporating elements of men's fashion, such as wide-brimmed hats and epaulettes. When both men and women began wearing heels, the heel and toe styles became gendered, as described above. By the early decades of the eighteenth century, it was no longer considered "masculine" for men to wear heels, as Enlightenment ideals that associated men with rational thought and women with sentiment deemed fashion a frivolous and feminine pursuit (Elizabeth Semmelhack, "Standing Tall: The Curious History of Men in Heels," from exhibition catalogue *Standing Tall: The Curious History of Men in Heels* [Toronto: Bata Shoe Museum Foundation, 2015], accessed June 11, 2018, https://artsandculture.google.com/exhibit/BQJSZR_j5AhtLA; Elizabeth Semmelhack quoted in William Kremer, "Why Did Men Stop Wearing High Heels?" BBC World Service, 25 January 2013, accessed June 11, 2018, https://www.bbc.com/news/magazine-21151350).

17. It should be noted that interpretation at Pilgrim Hall Museum is an ongoing process, and is updated when new information comes to light.

18. Ruth A. Bradford, "Historic Houses of Marshfield," *New England Magazine* 24 (1901): 427; Peggy M. Baker, "Vignettes from the Rogers Family: One Woman's Wardrobe," *Mayflower Quarterly* 81, no. 3 (September 2015): 237, 225–226.

19. Baker, "One Woman's Wardrobe," 233.

20. Baker, "One Woman's Wardrobe," 228.

21. Pilgrim Hall Museum Catalog Record 140. Insights about the purse were kindly provided by Susan North, Curator of Fashion 1550–1800, Victoria and Albert Museum (e-mail message to author, April 23, 2018), and by Lauren Whitley, Senior Curator of Textile and Fashion Arts, Museum of Fine Arts, Boston (e-mail message to author, June 4, 2018).

22. Loara Standish's sampler is housed at Pilgrim Hall Museum. For more information, see Peggy M. Baker, "Girlhood Embroidery," https://www.pilgrimhall.org/girlhood_embroidery.htm.

23. Pilgrim Hall Museum Catalog Record 145.1. Information about Margaret Howland's bodkin is from Baker, "One Woman's Wardrobe," 233. Penelope's bodkin has been at Pilgrim Hall Museum since the nineteenth century, when it was loaned by the "Misses Whitman" of Plymouth, Penelope's great-great-great-granddaughters (one of whom would name a son Herbert Pelham).

Insights about the bodkin were kindly provided by Nonie Gadsden, Katharine Lane Weems Senior Curator of American Decorative Arts and Sculpture, Museum of Fine Arts, Boston (e-mail message to author, June 13, 2018), and Beth Wees, Ruth Bigelow Wriston Curator of American Decorative Arts, Metropolitan Museum of Art (e-mail message to author, April 13, 2018).

For information on the important role bodkins played in the construction of personal identity in the seventeenth century, see Mary C. Beaudry, *Findings: The Material Culture of Needlework and Sewing* (New Haven: Yale University Press, 2007).

24. Finch, *Dissenting Bodies,* 113.

25. *Massachusetts: Vital Records, 1620–1850* (online database, AmericanAncestors.org, New England Historic Genealogical Society, 2001–2016): p. 5 lists the birth of Penelope and Josiah's unnamed daughter born in 1658, p. 3 lists her death two days later, and p. 6 records the births of Elizabeth and Edward.

26. John Demos, *A Little Commonwealth: Family Life in Plymouth Colony* (New York: Oxford University Press, 1970), 192; Karin Wulf, "Bible, King, and Common Law: Genealogical Literacies and Family History Practices in British America," *Early American Studies* 10, no. 3 (Fall 2012): 500, 470. Wulf's book-length work on this subject, tentatively titled "Lineage: Genealogy and the Power of Connection in Eighteenth-Century America," is forthcoming.

27. Insights on the dressing case were kindly provided by Nancy Carlisle, Senior Curator of Collections, Historic New England (e-mail message to author, April 16, 2018); Nonie Gadsden, Katharine Lane Weems Senior Curator of American Decorative Arts and Sculpture, Museum of Fine Arts, Boston (e-mail message to author, June 13, 2018); Nick Humphrey, Curator, Furniture Textiles, and Fashion, Victoria and Albert Museum (e-mail message to author, May 1, 2018); and Brock Jobe, Professor Emeritus, Office of Academic Programs, Winterthur Museum (e-mail message to author, June 4, 2018); Pilgrim Hall Museum Catalog Record 143.

28. Pilgrim Hall Museum Catalog Record 143.

29. Historic England, "Ferriers Farmhouse," https://www.historicengland.org.uk/listing/the-list/list-entry/1122879; probate inventory for Herbert Pelham, 2 July 1683, PROB32/24/98, transcript kindly provided to the author by Rebecca Fraser. Smallbridge Hall, like Ferriers, still stands, although it is not as large as it was during the time of Queen Elizabeth I's visit.

30. Bures St. Mary Baptisms, 1592–1660, transcribed from Suffolk Record Office Ref FL 540/4/2, fiche 3; https://essexandsuffolksurnames.co.uk/wp-content/uploads/2015/03/bures-st-mary-baptisms-1592-1660.pdf. The church of St. Mary in Bures still stands.

31. The colonists bought the land encompassing Cambridge and nearby Watertown from the "Squaw Sachem," widow of Massachusett tribal leader Nanapashemet. They paid the bargain price of £23 and the promise of a new coat every winter, which would have been considered by the sachem a form of tribute. (Information about the purchase of Cambridge land from "Brief History of Cambridge, Mass.," Cambridge Historical Commission, https://www.cambridgema.gov/historic/cambridgehistory; information about the Cambridge purchase and gifts to Natives being perceived as tributes from Brooks, *Our Beloved Kin,* 73, and Jenny Hale Pulsipher, *Swindler Sachem: The American Indian Who Sold His Birthright, Dropped*

Out of Harvard, and Conned the King of England [New Haven, Yale University Press, 2018], 98.)

32. Anne Bradstreet's book of poems, *The Tenth Muse Lately Sprung Up in America,* was first published in London in 1650 and in an expanded edition in Boston in 1678.

33. British National Archives Chancery Proceedings, Demurrer TNA/PRO: C5/14/109, 12, 13. (Thank you to Rebecca Fraser for the transcript in modern spelling.)

34. Details about the location of the Pelham houses are from *An Historic Guide to Cambridge* (Cambridge: Hannah Winthrop Chapter of the National Society of Daughters of the American Revolution, 1907), 33–35 and Samuel Eliot Morison, *The Founding of Harvard College* (Cambridge: Harvard University Press, 1935 reprint 1995), 328n3.

35. Richard R. Dunn, James Savage, and Laetitia Yeandle, eds., *The Journal of John Winthrop, 1630–1649* (Cambridge: Harvard University Press, 1996), 340.

36. For information about Herbert Pelham's landholdings: Roger Thompson, *Cambridge Cameos: Stories of Life in Seventeenth-Century New England* (Boston: New England Historic Genealogical Society, 2005), 18, 20.

37. "An Act for the Promoting and Propagating the Gospel of Jesus Christ in New England," July 27, 1649, in eds. C. H. Firth and R. S. Rait, *Acts and Ordinances of the Interregnum, 1642–1660,* (London, 1911), 197–200, *British History Online* (http:// www.british-history.ac.uk/no-series/acts-ordinances-interregnum/pp197-200). Harvard's Indian College, which was the campus's first building made of brick, the material historically associated with the college's architecture, closed before King Philip's War, in 1670, when the building was overtaken by the printing operation. Harvard renewed its outreach to Native Americans 300 years later, in 1970, with the creation of the Native American Program, designed to train leaders and educators; Peabody Museum of Anthropology and Ethnology, Harvard University, https:// www.peabody.harvard.edu/node/477, https://www.peabody.harvard.edu/node/2014, https://www.peabody.harvard.edu/node/2017.

38. Although John Langdon Sibley's *Biographical Sketches of Graduates of Harvard University* suggests Josiah was originally among the class of 1642, this is unlikely, since he would have been only fourteen years old (*Volume 1: The Classes of 1642–1658* [Cambridge: Charles William Sever, 1873], 16n1). More recent research has placed Josiah at Harvard in 1646 (James McLachlan, comp., "Non-Degree Students at Harvard College through the Class of 1690" [October 2003] in *Colonial Collegians, 1642–1774: Biographies of Those Who Attended American Colleges before the War for Independence* [Massachusetts Historical Society, New England Historic Genealogical Society, 2005, online database, AmericanAncestors.org, New England Historic Genealogical Society, 2008]).

39. Rebecca Fraser, *The Mayflower,* 190–192.

40. John Langdon Sibley, *Biographical Sketches of Graduates of Harvard University Volume 2: The Classes of 1659–1677* (Cambridge: Charles Sever, 1881), 416–420; Samuel G. Drake, transcriber, "Will of Herbert Pelham, Esq. 1672," *New England Historical and Genealogical Register* 18 (1864): 174.

41. The other half of Herbert Pelham's library was to go to Penelope's half-brother Edward; Penelope and Edward were to split Herbert's household possessions remaining in America.

42. After Herbert Pelham and Richard Saltonstall, who were both asked to return to England on colony business, declined the assignment, Edward Winslow took over the responsibility (Herbert Pelham and Richard Saltonstall to John Winthrop, November 17, 1646, and Herbert Pelham to John Winthrop, July 14, 1648, in Adam Winthrop, ed., *The Winthrop Papers,* vol. 5, 1645–1649 [Boston: Massachusetts Historical Society, 1947], 120; Fraser, *The Mayflower,* 228–229, 175).

43. Elizabeth Ward Saltonstall to Elizabeth Saltonstall, July 26, 1680, in Len Travers and Sheila McIntyre, *The Correspondence of John Cotton Junior* (Boston: The Colonial Society of Massachusetts, 2009), 265. The Saltonstalls were distantly related to Penelope.

44. John Winthrop, November 9, 1641, in Dunn, Savage, and Yaendle, eds., *The Journal of John Winthrop,* 192–193. On Penelope Pelham and Richard Bellingham having known each other in Boston, England, see Robert Charles Anderson, *Puritan Pedigrees: The Deep Roots of the Puritan Migration to New England* (Boston: New England Historic Genealogcal Society, 2018), 351.

45. Penelope Pelham Bellington voyaged to New England on May 15, 1635 (John Camden Hotten, ed., *Original Lists of Persons of Quality, 1600–1700* [London: published by the author, 1874; reprinted by Empire State Book Co., no date], 60); she became a member of the First Church of Boston in 1639 (New England Historic Genealogical Society, "The Records of the Churches of Boston," CD-ROM, 2002, "Boston, Mass. Church Records, 1630–1895" [online database, AmericanAncestors. org, New England Historic Genealogical Society, 2008], 13). Samuel Sewall's diary entry regarding Penelope Pelham Bellingham's death was made on May 29, 1702 (M. Halsey Thomas, ed., *The Diary of Samuel Sewall, 1674–1729* [New York: Farrar, Strauss, & Giroux, 1973], 1:468).

46. Quoted in Carla Gardina Pestana, *Quakers and Baptists in Colonial Massachusetts* (Cambridge: Cambridge University Press, 2004), 40; quoted in Samuel Walker, *Civil Liberties in America* (Santa Barbara, Calif.: ABC-CLIO, 2004), 148.

47. The description of the Bellingham house is from *A Volume of Records Relating to the Early History of Boston* 29 (Boston: Municipal Records Office, 1900), 184, and Edwin M. Bacon, *Boston: A Guide Book to the City and Vicinity* (Boston: Ginn and Co., 1922), 21. A surviving section of the house Richard Bellingham is supposed to have built as a "hunting lodge" in Chelsea, Massachusetts, now operates as the Governor Bellingham-Cary House museum.

48. *The City-State of Boston: The Rise and Fall of an Atlantic Power, 1630–1865* (Princeton: Princeton University Press, 2019), 31, 83.

49. There is a possibility Susanna was visiting Edward in London before he set sail; in a March 23, 1655 letter to Massachusetts governor John Winthrop, Roger Williams remarked upon Edward's departure for Hispaniola, "It is feared that his poor wife will miss him" (*Roger Williams Complete Writings: The Letters of Roger Williams,* vol 6 (reprint, Eugene, Oregon: Wipf & Stock Publishers, 2007), 288; W. Noel Sainsbury, ed. *Calendar of State Papers, Colonial America and West Indies,* vol. 1, 1574–1660 (originally published by Her Majesty's Stationery Office, London, 1860), https://www.british-history.ac.uk/cal-state-papers/colonial/america-west-indies/vol1/pp438-440. Recent research has revealed more about Susanna's background; see Sue Allan, Caleb Johnson, and Simon Neal, "The Origin of *Mayflower* Passenger Susanna (Jackson) (White) Winslow," *The American Genealogist* 89, no. 4 (Oct. 2017): 241–264.

50. For an exploration of this concept, see Mary Beth Norton, *Separated by Their Sex: Women in Public and Private in the Colonial Atlantic World* (Ithaca, N.Y.: Cornell University Press, 2011). Norton demonstrates how "public" and "private" spaces became gendered in the eighteenth century.

51. Alan MacFarlane, ed. *The Diary of Ralph Josselin, 1616–1683* (Oxford: Oxford University Press, 1991), entries for August 23, 1657 (406), September 30, 1657 (407), and May 7, 1657 (399). Information about Jemima's marriage to Samuel Kem was taken from Kem's parish registry notes as recorded in Joseph Lemuel Chester, "Herbert Pelham: His Ancestors and Descendants," *New England Historical and Genealogical Register* 33 (July 1879): 291. For the observation that Jemima may have been separated from her husband, see Fraser, *Mayflower,* 226.

52. Daniel Gookin, *Historical Collections of the Indians in New England* (Boston: Belknap and Hall, 1792), 62–63.

53. *Diary of Ralph Josselin,* October 12 and 10, 1658, 432.

54. Nathaniel Morton, *New England's Memorial,* 6th ed. (Boston: Congregational Board of Publication, 1855), 163, 172–174. Nathaniel Morton was Governor William Bradford's nephew.

55. Edward Johnson, *Wonder-Working Providence, or Sion's Savior in New England,* J. Franklin Jameson, ed., *Original Narratives of Early American History* (New York: Scribner's, 1910), 188.

56. Nathaniel Morton's *New England's Memorial* describes the challenges of the mid-seventeenth century. For an exploration of the jeremiad, see Sacvan Bercovitch, *The American Jeremiad* (Madison: University of Wisconsin Press, 1978, reprinted 2012); Virginia DeJohn Anderson, *New England's Generation: The Great Migration and the Formation of Society and Culture in the Seventeenth Century* (New York: Cambridge University Press, 1993), 209, 210.

57. The contract was signed July 27, 1662 (Nathaniel B. Shurtleff, ed. *The Records of the Colony of New Plymouth, Court Orders, 1661–1668* [New York: AMS Press, 1968], 4:69).

58. Laurel Thatcher Ulrich, *Good Wives: Image and Reality in the Lives of Women in Northern New England, 1650–1750* (New York: Vintage Books, 1991), 38, Thomas Fuller quoted p. 36; for an extended discussion of women's roles as deputy-husbands, see pp. 36–50.

59. Francis Baylies, *An Historical Memoir of the Colony of New Plymouth* (Boston: Hilliard, Gray, Little, & Wilkins, 1830), vol. 2 edited by Samuel G. Drake (Boston: Wiggin & Lunt, 1866), Part 4, 10; Pilgrim Hall Museum Catalog Record 55.

60. See, for example, Felicity Heal, *Hospitality in Early Modern England* (Oxford: Oxford University Press, 1990); Madeline Bassnett, *Women, Food Exchange, and Governance in Early Modern England* (New York: Palgrave McMillan, 2016); and Karin J. Goldstein, "The Creation of a New England Gentry: The Winslow Family of Plymouth Colony" (master's thesis, University of Massachusetts, Boston, 2001).

61. Rev. Samuel Angiers to Thomas Hinckley January 29, 1677, in "The Hinckley Papers," *Collections of the Massachusetts Historical Society,* ser. 4, 5: 12; Rev. Thomas Prince quoted in Nathaniel Morton, *New England's Memorial,* 5th ed., John Davis, ed. (Boston: Crocker and Brewster, 1826), 476n.

62. John Cotton mentions visits he and his wife paid to "Madam Winslow" in the 1690s (letters to Rowland Cotton, March 22, 1695, and August 16, 1695), in Travers and McIntyre, *The Correspondence of John Cotton Junior,* 25, 468, 483.

63. Mary C. Beaudry, Karin J. Goldstein, and Craig Chartier, "Archaeology of the Plymouth Colony in Massachusetts," *Avalon Chronicles* 8 (2003): 168.

64. Beaudry, Goldstein, and Chartier, 169, 172.

65. Gloria L. Main, "The Distribution of Consumer Goods in Colonial New England: A Subregional Approach," in *Early American Probate Inventories,* the Dublin Seminar for New England Folklife Annual Proceedings 1987, Peter Benes and Jane Montague Benes, eds. (Boston: Boston University, 1989), 160.

66. Josiah Winslow's will and inventory, *Plymouth Colony Records, Wills, 1633–1686,* 4:2:115–116 (will), 4:2:117 (inventory), www.familysearch.org; Pilgrim Society, *Catalog of the Historical Collections and Pictures in Pilgrim Hall, Plymouth* (1903), 34–35. For more information about Plymouth Colony libraries, see Jeremy Dupertuis Bangs, *Plymouth Colony's Private Libraries, as Recorded in Wills and Inventories, 1633–1692* (Leiden: Leiden American Pilgrim Museum, 2016).

67. George Ernest Bowman, transcriber, "Elizabeth (Tilley) Howland's Will," *Mayflower Descendant* 3 (1901): 55.

68. Josiah Winslow's inventory.

69. The plates are stylistically dated 1670–1680; two are at Pilgrim Hall Museum and one at the Massachusetts Historical Society (Goldstein, "The Creation of a New England Gentry," 84).

70. Pilgrim Hall Museum Catalog Record 944; Brian Cullity, *"A Cubberd, Four Joyne Stools & Other Smalle Thinges": The Material Culture of Plymouth Colony* (Sandwich, Mass.: Heritage Plantation, 1994), 128.

71. "A Genealogical Profile of John Winslow," Plimoth Plantation website, https://www.plimoth.org/sites/default/files/media/pdf/winslow_john.pdf.

72. Elizabeth ultimately did leave Penelope to marry Seth Arnold of Marshfield, but later commemorated their relationship by naming a daughter in her honor. *New England Marriages to 1700* (online database, AmericanAncestors.org, New England Historic Genealogical Society, 2008), 45; Massachusetts: Vital Records, 1620–1850 (online database, AmericanAncestors.org, New England Historic Genealogical Society, 2001–2016), 13.

73. Goldstein, "Creation of a New England Gentry," 103.

74. "The Last Will and Testament of John Jenney," Pilgrim Hall Museum website, https://www.pilgrimhall.org/pdf/John_Jenney_Will_Inventory.pdf. Penelope's brother Nathaniel had been a Harvard classmate of Charles Chauncy's sons Isaac and Ichabod.

75. July 22, 1634, *Records of the Colony of New Plymouth, Court Orders, 1637–1640,* 1:30.

76. *Records of the Colony of New Plymouth, Court Orders, 1651–1661,* 3:70, discussed in Demos, *A Little Commonwealth,* 111.

77. As Carole Shammas has explained, the great majority of individual households did not possess the skills or equipment necessary to produce the food, clothing, or other items they used, and records show that a significant number of goods were imported: "How Self-Sufficient Was Early America?" *The Journal of Interdisciplinary History* 13, no. 2 (Autumn 1982): 268.

78. Goldstein, 78; Josiah Winslow's will and inventory.

79. A similar comb from the same period was found in the Katherine Nanny Naylor archaeological site in Boston (Massachusetts Historical Commission, "Katherine Nanny Naylor: A Personal Story from Colonial Boston," http://www.sec.state.ma.us/mhc/mhcarchexhibitsonline/crossstreetbacklot.htm).

80. David B. Landon, "Feeding Colonial Boston: A Zooarchaeological Study," *Historical Archaeology* 3, no. 1 (1996): 34.

81. The seventeenth-century Hart Room from Ipswich, Mass. displayed at the Metropolitan Museum of Art includes a bed with dyed woolen hangings, https://www.metmuseum.org/about-the-met/curatorial-departments/the-american-wing/hart-room. For information on seventeenth-century bed hangings and the popularity

of crewelwork, see https://collections.vam.ac.uk/item/O78746/bed-hangings-pett-abigail/. For historical context on the tester bed, see http://collections.vam.ac.uk/item/O76345/tester-bed-unknown/.

82. "Collections and Exhibitions: 17th-Century Personal and Household Items," Pilgrim Hall Museum website, https://www.pilgrimhall.org/ce_17_century.htm; Jane Port, "Imported Pilgrim Pottery 101: Is Delftware from Delft? Is China from China?" Pilgrim Hall Museum website, https://www.pilgrimhall.org/pdf/Imported_Pilgrim_Pottery_101.pdf; Karin Goldstein, "Spoons, Salts, & Saucers: 300 Years of Table Settings," Pilgrim Hall Museum website, https://www.pilgrimhall.org/pdf/Spoons_Salts_Saucers.pdf. Goldstein, "A New England Gentry," 106. Kellie J. Bowers, "Native Interactions and Economic Exchange: A Re-Evaluation of Plymouth Colony Collections" (master's thesis, University of Massachusetts, Boston, 2015), 44, 126. Shell middens found on the site point to an earlier occupation by Native peoples (Beaudry, Goldstein, and Chartier, "Archaeology of the Plymouth Colony in Massachusetts," 165). Insight into Penelope possibly using Native pots was kindly provided by then-Plimoth Plantation curator Kate Ness, personal meeting on April 23, 2018.

83. Christa M. Beranek, David B. Landon, John M. Steinberg, and Brian Damiata, editors, "Project 400: The Plymouth Colony Archaeological Survey Report on the 2016 Field Season Cole's Hill, Brewster Garden, and Burial Hill, Plymouth, Massachusetts," University of Massachusetts Boston Andrew Fiske Memorial Center for Archaeological Research, Cultural Resource Management Study No. 77 August 2017; Bowers, "Native Interactions," 132.

84. Bowers, "Native Interactions," 83, 86; Katherine Howlett Hayes, Stephen Silliman, and Elizabeth Kiniry (Karin J. Goldstein, contributor), "Initial Survey and Identification of Archaeological Resources at the Historic Winslow House in Marshfield, Massachusetts" (University of Massachusetts, Boston, Center for Environmental History, 2004), 12, Appendix A.

85. Edward Bell, John and Priscilla Alden Family Sites, National Historic Landmark Nomination, 2008, 48, 50, 52.

86. Rebecca Fraser, "Discussion of Previously Unpublished 1656 Memorandum of Josiah Winslow at the Massachusetts Historical Society," *Mayflower Journal* 1 no. 2 (Fall 2016): 29–38. Documents associated with the estate of Josiah's sister Elizabeth's husband George Corwin note that some linens belonging to her were being stored at Marshfield, but these likely would not have been listed among Josiah's belongings on the probate inventory. The iron Josiah exported was likely from the Saugus Iron Works established by John Winslow, Jr., for which Josiah served as an agent for English investors. The ship Josiah references in the Memorandum was also carrying Penelope's brother Nathaniel, and was lost at sea.

87. William Bradford, *Of Plymouth Plantation, 1620–1647* (New York: Modern Library, 1981), 198; Eric J. Dolin, *Fur, Fortune, and Empire: The Epic History of the*

Fur Trade in America (New York: W. W. Norton, 2010), 55, 84.

88. Beaudry, Goldstein, and Chartier, "The Archaeology of the Plymouth Colony in Massachusetts," 178. (Edward Winslow imported the first cattle to New England in 1624, providing an important food source for Plymouth Colony.)

89. Wendy Warren, *New England Bound: Slavery and Colonization in Early America* (New York: Liveright, 2016), 11.

90. Richard Vines to John Winthrop, July 19, 1647, in Allyn B. Forbes, ed., *Winthrop Papers* 5:172.

91. Warren, *New England Bound,* 52–53.

92. Warren, *New England Bound,* 104.

93. Hope's indenture is in Winthrop Papers, 5:196–197. Margaret Ellen Newell, *Brethren by Nature: New England Indians, Colonists, and the Origins of American Slavery* (Ithaca: Cornell University Press, 2016), 58–59.

94. *Records of the Colony of New Plymouth, Court Orders, 1661–1668,* 4:18–19. *Plymouth Colony Deeds, 1671–1673* (online database, AmericanAncestors.org, New England Historic Genealogical Society, 2019), vol. 3, part 2, 70 (Joseph Bumpas to Nathaniel Thomas, June 26, 1672).

95. *Plymouth Colony Deeds, 1671–1673,* vol. 3, part 2, 62–64 (Tuspaquin and Mantowapact to Edward Gray and Josiah Winslow, June 30, 1672).

96. For more information on the Winslows' relationships with Plymouth Colony Natives, see Fraser, *The Mayflower.*

97. Jill Lepore, *The Name of War: King Philip's War and the Origins of American Identity* (New York: Knopf, 1998), xi.

98. It is possible some of the undated Native-made stone items found on the property, such as projectile points and pestles, date from this period.

99. Brooks, *Our Beloved Kin,* 2–4, 34.

100. Yasuhide Kawashima, *Igniting King Philip's War: The John Sassamon Murder Trial* (Lawrence: University Press of Kansas, 2001), 1, 85.

101. *Records of the Colony of New Plymouth, Court Orders, 1668–1678,* 5:168; Kawashima, *Igniting King Philip's War,* 102, 103.

102. Kawashima, *Igniting King Philip's War,* 129.

103. Josiah Winslow to John Leverett, June 28, 1675, and June 21, 1675, Josiah Winslow to John Freeman, June 28, 1675; Josiah Winslow to James Cudworth, July 18, 1675, Winslow Papers, Massachusetts Historical Society; Josiah Winslow to James Cudworth, June 27, 1675, and Josiah Winslow to John Leverett, July 6,

1675, Josiah Winslow Papers, Boston Athenaeum; Josiah Winslow to James Cudworth, July 6, 1675, Winslow Papers, MHS; Lepore, *The Name of War*, xi.

104. Quoted in James Thacher, *History of the Town of Plymouth* (Boston: Marsh, Capen, and Lyon, 1835), 140; Josiah Winslow to Thomas Prence, March 24, 1671, Winslow Papers, MHS, quoted in Pulsipher, *Subjects unto the Same King*, 94–95.

105. Beaudry, Goldstein, and Chartier, "The Archaeology of the Plymouth Colony in Massachusetts," 171–172.

106. A 1683 letter written by an Elizabeth Corwin in the Corwin manuscripts collection at the Peabody Essex Museum's Phillips Library mentions the author's mother, but the writer does not appear to have been Elizabeth Winslow Brooks Corwin.

107. Jonathan Corwin's house still stands in Salem and operates as a museum called "The Witch House." For information on the legal battle over George Corwin's estate pressed by Jonathan Corwin against Elizabeth Winslow Corwin, see Fraser, *Mayflower*, Chapter 19. For information about Salem's fortifications: Emerson W. Baker, *A Storm of Witchcraft: The Salem Trials and the American Experience* (New York: Oxford University Press, 2015), 50–51.

108. George M. Bodge, *Soldiers in King Philip's War* (Boston: Printed for the author, 1891), 320; Kyle F. Zelner, *A Rabble in Arms: Massachusetts Towns and Militiamen during King Philip's War* (New York: New York University Press, 2009), 57.

109. Rev. John Cotton junior to Rev. Thomas Walley, February 4, 1676, in Travers and McIntyre, *Correspondence of John Cotton Junior*, 134; Lepore, *The Name of War*, 103–104.

110. Josiah Cotton, "Supplement to New England's Memorial," in Nathaniel Morton, *New England's Memorial*, 6th ed., 226.

111. N[athaniel] S[altonstall], *A New and Further Narrative of the State of New England* (London: Printed by F. B. for Dorman Newman, 1676), in Charles H. Lincoln, ed., *Narratives of the Indian Wars, 1675–1699* (New York: Scribner's, 1913), 80; N[athaniel] S[altonstall], *A Continuation of the state of New-England being a farther account of the Indian warr, and of the engagement betwixt the joynt forces of the United English collonies and the Indians on the 19th of December 1675…* (London: Printed by T. M. for Dorman Newman, 1676), 15.

112. Thomas Hinckley to Mary Hinckley, February 10, 1676, in "The Hinckley Papers," *Collections of the Massachusetts Historical Society*, ser. 4, 5:1–2.

113. Mary Herendean Pray to Captain James Oliver, October 20, 1675, in Sharon M. Harris, ed., *American Women Writers to 1850* (New York: Oxford University Press, 1996), 184–187.

114. Josiah Cotton, "Supplement to New England's Memorial," in Nathaniel

Morton, *New England's Memorial,* 226.

115. Josiah himself benefited directly in some ways from the sale of Indian captives, as the Plymouth General Court reimbursed him for expenses he had incurred during the summer of 1675 from "the prise of ten Indians, of those salvages lately transported out of the gov^rment" (*Records of the Colony of New Plymouth, Court Orders, 1668–1678,* 5:175). Also, Josiah and the "Councill" gave his sister Elizabeth Winslow Brooks Corwin an Indian boy, which her husband George later sold (Estate of Captain George Corwin, Essex County Court Papers 44:96, in Susan E. Roser, *Mayflower Deeds and Probates from the Files of George Ernest Bowman at the Massachusetts Society of Mayflower Descendants* (Genealogical Publishing 1994), 548. For an estimation of the number of women and children killed in the burning of the Narragansett fort, Brooks, *Our Beloved Kin,* 244.

116. For two important recent works on perceiving King Philip's War from a Native perspective, see Lisa Brooks, *Our Beloved Kin: A New History of King Philip's War* (New Haven: Yale University Press, 2018) and Christine DeLucia, *Memory Lands: King Philip's War and the Place of Violence in the Northeast* (New Haven, Yale University Press, 2018); Boston Harbor islands internment statistic from *Memory Lands,* 52–53.

117. DeLucia, *Memory Lands,* 143–144.

118. Josiah Winslow to John Leverett, July 6, 1675, Winslow Papers, MHS.

119. Quotes from Josiah Winslow in Increase Mather, *A Brief History of the War with the Indians in New England* (Boston: John Foster, 1676), online electronic text edition, Paul Royster ed., DigitalCommons@University of Nebraska, Lincoln, 82–83.

120. Josiah Winslow to King Charles, June 26, 1677, *Calendar of State Papers Colonial, America and West Indies: 1677–1680* (originally published by Her Majesty's Stationery Office, London, 1896), 10:99–110, no. 314, https://www.british-history.ac.uk/cal-state-papers/colonial/america-west-indies/vol10/pp99-110. Wampanoag scholar Paula Peters is currently pursuing the whereabouts of Metacom's wampum belts in conjunction with an exhibit on the construction of a new wampum belt by artisans of the Wampanoag nation featuring a series of short films.

121. George D. Langdon, Jr., *Pilgrim Colony: A History of New Plymouth, 1620–1691* (New Haven: Yale University Press, 1966), 188–189.

122. Edward Randolph to King Charles II, September 20, 1676, in *Edward Randolph,* vol 2. (Boston: Printed for the Prince Society, 1898), 122. For Randolph staying with Josiah and Penelope for a "sevennight" in December: William Bradford junior to Rev. John Cotton junior, December 20, 1679, in Travers and McIntyre, *Correspondence of John Cotton Junior,* 255. In a letter to Josiah dated January 29, 1679/80, Randolph remarked that he and the Winslows' friends at Salem had "solemnly remembered" Josiah "and lady" once a day, and sent his "humble thanks

for all and last favours" (printed in *Collections of the Massachusetts Historical Society for the Year 1799* 6, ser. 1 (reprint, Boston: Charles Little & James Brown, 1846), 92–94. William Blathwayt's Whitehall communication to Josiah Winslow, February 29, 1680, in "The Hinckley Papers," 5: 32, 34.

123. E. Jennifer Monaghan, *Learning to Read and Write in Colonial America* (Amherst: University of Massachusetts Press, 2005), 15.

124. William Avery to Josiah Winslow, 1673, Winslow Papers, MHS; Rev. Samuel Arnold to Rev. John Cotton junior, April 4, 1677, Travers and McIntyre, *The Correspondence of John Cotton Junior*, 191–192.

125. *Diary of Samuel Sewall*, December 18, 1680, 47.

126. Goldstein, "The Creation of a New England Gentry," 106; Travers and McIntyre, *The Correspondence of John Cotton Junior*, 490–492.

127. *Records of the Colony of New Plymouth, Court Orders, 1678–1691*, 6:63.

128. Quote about Harvard commencement from letter of John Cotton to Thomas Hinckley, August 16, 1681, in Travers and McIntyre, *The Correspondence of John Cotton Junior*, 278; Thomas Hinckley, "Upon the Death of the Honourable and Highly Esteemed Josiah Winslow," in "The Hinckley Papers," 53; William Witherell, "Upon the Much To Be Lamented Death of the Thrice Three Times Honored Josiah Winslow…," reprinted in Samuel Deane, *History of Scituate to 1831* (Boston: James Loring, 1831), 395–397; Josiah Cotton, "Supplement to New England's Memorial," 226.

129. Will of Josiah Winslow. For more on widowhood in colonial America, see Vivian Bruce Conger, *The Widow's Might: Widowhood and Gender in Early British America* (New York: New York University Press, 2009). Penelope's aunt Penelope Bellingham herself lived for thirty years as a former governor's widow following Richard Bellingham's death in 1672.

130. Nathaniel Morton to Penelope Winslow, December 28, 1680, Winslow Family Papers, MHS; Robert F. Trent, "Arms and Armor," in *New England Begins: The Seventeenth Century*, vol. 1 (Museum of Fine Arts Boston, 1982), 53; Steven C. Bullock, "'Often Concerned in Funerals': Ritual, Material Culture, and the Large Funeral in the Age of Samuel Sewall," in Martha J. MacNamara and Georgia B. Barnhill, eds., *New Views of New England: Studies in Visual and Material Culture, 1680–1830*, vol. 82 (Boston: Publications of the Colonial Society, 2012).

131. Insights about the mourning ring were generously provided by Nonie Gadsden, Katharine Lane Weems Senior Curator of American Decorative Arts and Sculpture, Museum of Fine Arts, Boston (e-mail message to author, June 13, 2018), and Beth Wees, Ruth Bigelow Wriston Curator of American Decorative Arts, Metropolitan Museum of Art (e-mail message to author, April 2, 2018). (Nonie Gadsden also consulted with Gerald Ward and Barbara McLean Ward.) The mourning ring

and purse were loaned to Pilgrim Hall Museum in 1882 by Mary Chilton Hayward Mitchell, who appears to have been a Winslow descendant, and they have been at the museum ever since.

132. Nathaniel Morton to Penelope Winslow, December 28, 1680, Winslow Papers, MHS.

133. Rev. John Cotton junior to Mary Smith Glover Hinckley, January 10, 1684, in Travers and McIntyre, *The Correspondence of John Cotton Junior,* 296–297; Herbert Pelham to John Winthrop, April 3, 1648, quoted in Francis J. Bremer, *John Winthrop: America's Forgotten Founding Father* (New York: Oxford University Press, 2003), 372–373.

134. Nathaniel Morton to Penelope Winslow, December 28, 1680, Winslow Papers, MHS; Nathaniel Morton to Penelope Winslow, undated, Boston Athenaeum, Josiah Winslow Papers, Mss. L461.

135. Nathaniel Morton to Penelope Winslow, undated, Boston Athenaeum, Josiah Winslow Papers, Mss. L461

136. Ibid.

137. *Diary of Ralph Josselin,* June 29, 1674, 577.

138. Demos, *A Little Commonwealth,* 192.

139. For the establishment of Bristol, *Records of the Colony of New Plymouth, Court Orders, 1678–1691,* 6:77; for the Burtons' marriage date, *Rhode Island: Vital Records, 1636–1850,* 6:11 (online database, AmericanAncestors.org, New England Historic Genealogical Society, 2014).

140. *Rhode Island: Vital Records, 1636–1850*; August 8, 1694 quote from inventory of John Smith senior of Taunton, "Abstract from the First Book of Bristol County Probate Records," *The Genealogical Advertiser* 4 (1901): 125.

141. *Rhode Island: Vital Records, 1636–1850,* 1:67 for births of Penelope and Thomas.

142. "The Last Will and Testament of Samuel Fuller," Pilgrim Hall Museum website, https://www.pilgrimhall.org/pdf/Samuel_Fullers_Will_Inventory.pdf; Travers and McIntyre, *The Correspondence of John Cotton Junior,* 449n1.

143. The quote about Elizabeth Pelham's age is taken from her gravestone.

144. Penelope Winslow Deed to Joseph Church, November 5, 1685, *Bristol County Deeds* 7:521; Penelope Winslow Deed to Elizabeth Burton, May 4, 1688, *Bristol County Deeds* 6:311–312. Perhaps Penelope, like Josiah, had a seal ring bearing her family's coat of arms.

145. Beaudry, Goldstein, and Chartier, "The Archaeology of the Plymouth Colony in Massachusetts," 171.

146. Demos, *A Little Commonwealth,* 98; Finch, *Dissenting Bodies,* 110.

147. For more information about this transition in Plymouth Colony, see Cynthia Hagar Krusell, *Plymouth Colony to Plymouth County: The Land, the Church, the People, 1680–1690* (Marshfield, Mass.: Pondside Publishing, 2010), and Langdon, *Pilgrim Colony,* 224–240.

148. At the time of Herbert Pelham's death, Ralph Josselin noted in his diary that Herbert "was as noteles to good[,] yett minded some litle other little things. I commended him to god. lord what is man," June 29, 1674, 577.

149. Penelope Winslow Deposition, National Archives, London, Document C8/338/282, transcribed by Rebecca Fraser in "Penelope Pelham and a Taste for Litigation," *Mayflower Quarterly* 81, no. 3 (September 2015): 241–244. In discovering this petition, Fraser was able to draw the conclusion that Penelope had never moved back to England with her family, overturning previous assumptions.

150. Rev. John Cotton junior to Rowland Cotton, March 22, 1695, Travers and McIntyre, *The Correspondence of John Cotton Junior,* 468. For an extended discussion of the Pelham inheritance cases, see Fraser, *The Mayflower,* 291, 296–299, 309–311.

151. Deposition of Joseph Dudley, November 14, 1698, High Court of Chancery, C22/998/33. Dudley was testifying on behalf of Edward Pelham in Edward's suit against Waldegrave.

152. Penelope Winslow Petition, June 30, 1703, *Massachusetts Archives Collection* (Felt Collection) 45: 296.

153. Deeds Edward Pelham witnessed for Josiah, when an assistant governor, on July 30, 1672, and June 1, 1673, indicate that he may have been living with the Winslows during Harvard's summer breaks (*Plymouth Colony Deeds, 1671–1673* vol. 3, part 2, 74, 162).

154. Isaac Winslow to John Winslow, *Plymouth County Deed Records, 1725–1726,* 20:35.

155. *Plymouth County, Mass.: Plymouth Court Records, 1686–1859* (online database, AmericanAncestors.org, New England Historic Genealogical Society, 2008), 6:228 (appearing in database 1:82) and 7:3–5 (appearing in database 2:3).

156. James Deetz, *In Small Things Forgotten: The Archaeology of Early American Life* (New York: Anchor Books, 1977), 72, 78.

157. Susan Smith, "Stephen Burton of Bristol, R.I., and Some of His Descendants," *New England Historical and Genealogical Register* 60 (Jan. 1906), 29; Bristol County Deeds, 13:372.

158. For Thomas as a school teacher, Henry Litchfield, *Ancient Landmarks of Pembroke* (Pembroke: George Edward Lewis, 1909), 69; for Thomas as Pembroke's

town clerk, "Pembroke, Mass. Births, Marriages, and Deaths," in *The Genealogical Advertiser* (June 1898): 1.

159. Edward Winslow to John Winslow, August 7, 1746, Pilgrim Hall Museum transcript. In her 1753 will, Sarah left "the four pictures" (the three Winslow paintings and the one of her mother, Elizabeth Paddy Wensley) to her son John, who inherited the house (Docket #23223, Plymouth County Probate Records, 1751–1755, 13:201).

160. Finch and Rose, Preservation Consultants, Isaac Winslow House Architectural Conditions Assessment, 2016, 1–2, 18–19.

161. *Colonial Collegians, 1642–1774: Biographies of Those Who Attended American Colleges before the War for Independence* (online database, AmericanAncestors.org, New England Historic Genealogical Society, 2008), 2558, 2559.

162. Isaac Winslow to Penelope Winslow Warren, July 1, 1737, Ms. S-208, Winslow Papers, MHS.

163. Quoted in "Memoir of the Descendants of Edward Winslow," *New England Historical and Genealogical Register* 4 (Oct. 1850): 302.

164. Will and inventory of Isaac Winslow, Docket #23184, *Plymouth County Probate Records, 1738–1742*, 8: 27 (will) and 29 (inventory).

165. *Suffolk Court Files, 1700–1714*, 270.

166. "List of Servants for Life within the Town of Marshfield" in the Massachusetts 1754 slave census; Marshfield Town Records, March 17, 1788, 227; Karin J. Goldstein, "Parlors and Garrets: The Winslow Families and Their Servants," *The Mayflower Quarterly* 64, no. 4 (November 1998): 322.

167. Jared Leonard, "Exhibiting Archaeology," Society for Historical Archaeology website, www.sha.org/research/exhibiting_archaeology_article.cfm; "Director's Note, Fall 2016," Newport Historical Society website, https://newporthistory.org/directors-note-fall-2016/.

168. Cynthia Hagar Krusell, *Of Tea and Tories: The Story of Revolutionary Marshfield* (Marshfield Bicentennial Committee, 1976), 6.

169. *Colonial Collegians, 1642–1774: Biographies of Those Who Attended American Colleges before the War for Independence*, 5933; Krusell, *Of Tea and Tories*, 7.

170. Krusell, *Of Tea and Tories*, 5–6.

171. Benjamin Marston, diary, 1776–1787 (University of New Brunswick, Benjamin Marston Diary Project), December 14, 1776. Thank you to Peggy Baker for bringing this poem to my attention.

172. James Thacher, *History of Plymouth*, 143.

173. For an exploration of the factors driving colonists to become revolutionaries or remain Loyalists, see Virginia DeJohn Anderson, *The Martyr and the Traitor: Nathan Hale, Moses Dunbar, and the American Revolution* (New York: Oxford University Press, 2017); Julie Hardwick, Sarah M. S. Pearsall, and Karin Wulf, "Introduction: Centering Families in Atlantic Histories," *William and Mary Quarterly* 70, no. 2 (April 2013): 205–224.

Index

About the Author

Michelle Marchetti Coughlin is an independent scholar and the author of *One Colonial Woman's World: The Life and Writings of Mehetabel Chandler Coit,* which received an honorable mention for the Western Association of Women Historians' 2014 Penny Kanner Prize. Ms. Coughlin has been a Mass Humanities Scholar in Residence and a historical consultant, and in 2019 guest-curated Pilgrim Hall Museum's *pathFOUNDERS: Women of Plymouth* exhibit. She currently serves on the Board of the Abigail Adams Birthplace and as Museum Administrator of Boston's Gibson House Museum. She maintains a website at www.onecolonialwomansworld.com.